RENÉ GUÉNON

THE CRISIS
OF THE
MODERN WORLD

THE CRISIS OF THE MODERN WORLD

PREFACE

When, a few years ago, we wrote East and West, we
thought we had given all the information we needed, at least
for the time being, on the questions that were the subject of
this book. Since then, events have moved with ever-increasing speed, and without making us change a single word of
what we said then, they have made certain additional clarifications timely, and led us to develop points of view on which
we had not thought it necessary to insist at the outset. These
clarifications are all the more necessary as we have recently
witnessed the re-assertion, in a rather aggressive form, of
some of the confusions that we have already endeavoured to
dispel; while carefully refraining from getting involved in
any polemics, we have seen fit to set the record straight once
again. There are, in this order, considerations, even elemen-
tary ones, which seem so foreign to the vast majority of our
contemporaries, that, in order to make them understand, we
must not tire of coming back to them again and again, presenting them under their different aspects, and explaining
more fully, as circumstances allow, what can give rise to difficulties that it was not always possible to foresee at the outset.

The very title of this volume calls for a few explanations, which we must provide first of all, so that it is clear how we understand it, and that there can be no ambiguity in this respect. That we can speak of a crisis in the modern world, taking the word "crisis" in its most ordinary sense, is something that many people no longer doubt, and in this respect at least, there has been a fairly noticeable change: under the very influence of events, certain illusions are beginning to dissipate, and for our part, we can only welcome this, for it is, in spite of everything, a rather favorable symptom, an indication of the possibility of a turnaround in contemporary mentality, something that appears as a faint glimmer in the midst of the current chaos. For example, the belief in indefinite "progress", once held as a kind of intangible, indisputable dogma, is no longer so generally accepted; some people have a vague, more or less confused idea that Western civilization, instead of continuing to develop in the same direction, could one day come to a standstill, or even sink entirely in some cataclysm. Perhaps these people don't see the danger clearly, and the fanciful or childish fears they sometimes express are proof enough of the persistence of many errors in their minds; But it's already something that they realize that there is a danger, even if they feel it more than they really understand it, and that they manage to conceive that this civilization of which moderns are so infatuated does not occupy a privileged place in the history of the world, that it may have the same fate as so many others that have already disappeared in more or less distant times, some of which have left behind them only minute traces, barely perceptible or barely recognizable vestiges.

So, if we say that the modern world is undergoing a crisis, what we most usually mean is that it has reached a critical point, or, in other words, that a more or less profound

4

transformation is imminent, that a change of direction will inevitably have to take place in the near future, willingly or unwillingly, more or less abruptly, with or without catastrophe. This understanding is perfectly legitimate, and corresponds to part of what we ourselves think, but only part, because for us, and from a more general point of view, the whole of the modern era represents a period of crisis for the world; it seems, moreover, that we are nearing the end, and this is what makes the abnormal nature of this state of affairs, which has lasted for several centuries, but whose consequences have not yet been as visible as they are now, more sensitive today than ever before. This is also why events are unfolding with the accelerated speed to which we alluded at the outset; no doubt, it can go on like this for some time yet, but not indefinitely; and even, without being able to assign a precise limit, we have the impression that it can't go on much longer.

But the very word "crisis" contains other meanings, making it even more apt to express what we want to say: its etymology, in fact, which is often lost sight of in common usage, but to which we should refer as we always must when we want to restore to a term the fullness of its proper meaning and original value, its etymology, we say, makes it partly synonymous with "judgment" and "discrimination". The phase that can be said to be truly "critical", in any order of things, is the one that immediately leads to a favorable or unfavorable solution, the one in which a decision is made in one direction or the other; it is then, therefore, that it is possible to pass judgment on the results acquired, to weigh the "pros" and the "cons", operating a sort of ranking among these results, some positive, others negative, and to see which way the scales tip definitively. Of course, we have no pretension of establishing such a complete discrimination, which would be premature, since the crisis has not yet been resolved, and it is perhaps not even possible to say exactly when and how it will be, especially since it is always preferable to refrain from certain predictions which cannot be based on reasons clearly intelligible to all, and which, consequently, would be too likely to be misinterpreted and add to the confusion instead of remedying it. All we can propose to do, then, is to contribute, to a certain extent and as far as the means at our disposal will allow, to making those who are capable of doing so aware of some of the results which now seem to be well established, and thus to prepare, if only in a very partial and rather indirect way, the elements which will later serve as the basis for the future "judgement", from which a new period in the history of terrestrial mankind will open up.

Some of the expressions we have just used will undoubtedly evoke, in the minds of some, the idea of what is known as the "Last Judgment", and, to be honest, this will not be wrong; whether it is meant literally or symbolically, or in both ways at the same time, as they are by no means mutually exclusive in reality, is of little importance here, and this is neither the time nor the place to explain ourselves fully on this point. In any case, this weighing up of "for" and "against", this discrimination of positive and negative results, which we were talking about earlier, can certainly make us think of the division of the "chosen" and the "damned" into two immutably fixed groups from now on; even if this is only an analogy, we must recognize that it is at least a valid and well-founded one, in conformity with the very nature of things; and this calls for a few more explanations.

It's no coincidence that so many people today are haunted by the idea of the "end of the world"; This is regrettable in some respects, for the extravagances to which this misunderstood idea gives rise, the "messianic" ramblings that are its consequence in various circles, all these manifestations of the mental imbalance of our time, only serve to aggravate this same imbalance to a degree that is not absolutely negligible; but it is no less certain that this is a fact that cannot be ignored. The most convenient attitude, when things of this kind come to light, is undoubtedly that of simply dismissing them without further examination, treating them as errors or unimportant daydreams; We believe, however, that even if they are indeed errors, it would be better, while denouncing them as such, to investigate the reasons that gave rise to them, and the more or less distorted part of the truth that may be contained in them in spite of everything, for, since error has, after all, only a purely negative mode of existence, absolute error can be found nowhere and is merely an empty word. If we look at things in this way, we can easily see that this preoccupation with the "end of the world" is closely linked to the general state of unease in which we live at present: the obscure presentiment of something that is indeed close to ending, acting uncontrollably on certain imaginations, quite naturally produces disordered, and more often than not crudely materialized, representations which, in turn, translate outwardly into the extravagances to which we have just alluded. This explanation is no excuse for these extravagances; or at least, if we can excuse those who involuntarily fall into error, because they are predisposed to it by a mental state for which they are not responsible, this can never be a reason to excuse the error itself. We know that some people would even be tempted to reproach us with the opposite, and perhaps what we say here will help them better understand how we approach these things, striving always to place ourselves in the only point of view that matters to us, that of impartial and disinterested truth.

And that's not all: a merely "psychological" explanation of the idea of the "end of the world" and its current manifestations, however correct it may be in its order, would not be fully sufficient in our eyes; to stop there would be to allow ourselves to be influenced by one of those modern illusions against which we protest on every occasion. Some people, we say, have a confused sense of the imminent end of something whose nature and scope they cannot exactly define ; it must be admitted that they have a very real perception of this, albeit vague and subject to misinterpretation or imaginative distortion, since, whatever this end may be, the crisis that must inevitably lead to it is quite apparent, and a multitude of unequivocal and easily observed signs all lead concordantly to the same conclusion. If what must come to an end is Western civilization in its present form, it is understandable that those who have become accustomed to seeing nothing outside it, to considering it as "civilization" without an epithet, should easily believe that everything will come to an end with it, and that, if it disappears, it will truly be the "end of the world".

To put things into perspective, we would say that we are indeed approaching the end of a world, i.e. the end of an epoch or historical cycle, which may also correspond to a cosmic cycle, as all traditional doctrines teach. There have already been many events of this kind in the past, and no doubt there will be others in the future; events of unequal importance, moreover, depending on whether they bring to an end more or less extended periods and whether they concern the whole of terrestrial humanity, or only one or other of its portions, a particular race or people. In the present state of the world, it is to be assumed that the change that will take place will be very general in scope, and that whatever form it may take, and which we do not intend to attempt to define, it will affect the whole earth to a greater or lesser extent. In any case, the laws governing such events are applicable analogously to all degrees; so this which is said of the "end of the world", in a sense as complete as it is possible to conceive it, and which moreover usually refers only to the terrestrial world, is still true, all things considered, when it is simply a question of the end of any world, understood in a much more restricted sense.

It may be difficult to give a full account of these laws in a form easily accessible to Western minds, but it is at least necessary to have some data on the subject if we are to form a true idea of what the present epoch is and what it exactly represents in the whole of world history. This is why we will begin by showing that the characteristics of this epoch are indeed those which traditional doctrines have always indicated for the cyclical period to which it corresponds; and it will also be to show that what is anomaly and disorder at a certain point of view is nevertheless a necessary element of a larger order, an inevitable consequence of the laws which govern the development of all manifestation. On the contrary, it's a reason to work as hard as we can to prepare the way out of this "dark age", whose more or less imminent, if not quite imminent, end we can already glimpse. This, too, is in order, for equilibrium is the result of the simultaneous action of two opposing tendencies; if either of them could cease to act altogether , equilibrium would never be restored, and the world itself would vanish ; But this supposition is impractical, for the two terms of an opposition only make sense through each other, and, whatever the appearances, we can be sure that all partial and transitory imbalances ultimately contribute to the achievement of total equilibrium.

CHAPTER I

THE DARK AGE

Hindu doctrine teaches that the duration of a human cycle, to which it gives the name of *Manvantara*, is divided into four ages, which mark as many phases of a gradual darkening of primordial spirituality; these are the same periods that the traditions of Western antiquity, for their part, referred to as the Ages of Gold, Silver, Bronze and Iron. We are now in the fourth age, the *Kali-Yuga* or "Dark Age", and have been in it, it is said, for over six thousand years, that is to say, for a period far earlier than any known to "classical" history. Since then, the truths that were once accessible to all men have become more and more hidden and difficult to reach; those who possess them are fewer and fewer, and while the treasure of "non-human" wisdom, which predates all ages, can never be lost, it is wrapped in increasingly impenetrable veils, which conceal it from view and under which it is extremely difficult to discover. This is why it is everywhere spoken of, in various symbols, as something that has been lost, at least in appearance and in relation to the outside world, and which must be found by those who aspire to true knowledge; but it is also said that what is thus hidden will become visible again at the end of this cycle, which will at the same time, by virtue of the continuity that links all things together, be the beginning of a new cycle.

But, it may be asked, why must cyclical development take place in such a downward direction, from the higher to the lower, which, as will be readily observed, is the very negation of the idea of "progress" as understood by modernists? This is because the development of any manifestation necessarily implies an ever-increasing distance from the principle from which it proceeds; starting from the highest point, it necessarily tends downwards, and, like heavy bodies, it tends there with ever-increasing speed, until it finally comes to a standstill. This fall could be characterized as a progressive materialization, for the expression of the principle is pure spirituality; we say the expression, not the principle itself, for it cannot be designated by any of the terms that seem to indicate any opposition, being beyond all oppositions. Moreover, words like "spirit" and "matter", which we borrow from Western language for convenience, have little more than symbolic value for us; In any case, they can only be truly appropriate to what we're talking about if we set aside the special interpretations given to them by modern philosophy, of which "spiritualism" and "materialism" are, in our eyes, only two complementary forms which imply each other and which are equally negligible for those who wish to rise above these contingent points of view. But then, it is not pure metaphysics that we propose to deal with here, and that is why, without ever losing sight of the essential principles, we can, while taking the necessary precautions to avoid any equivocation, allow ourselves the use of terms which, although inadequate, seem likely to make things more easily understandable, insofar as this can be done without distorting them.

What we've just said about the development of manifestation presents a view which, while accurate overall, is nevertheless over-simplified and schematic, in that it may lead us to believe that this development takes place in a straight line, in a single direction and without oscillations of any kind; the reality is far more complex. In fact, as we pointed out earlier, there are two opposing tendencies in all things, one descending and the other ascending, or, to use another mode of representation, "centrifugal" and "centrifugal", one centrifugal and the other centripetal, and from the predominance of one or the other proceed two complementary phases of manifestation, one away from the principle, the other back towards it, which are often symbolically compared to the movements of the heart or the two phases of breathing. Although these two phases are usually described as successive, it must be understood that, in reality, the two tendencies to which they correspond always act simultaneously, albeit in varying proportions; and it sometimes happens, at certain critical moments when the downward tendency seems on the point of winning out definitively in the general march of the world, that a special action intervenes to reinforce the opposite tendency, so as to re-establish a certain balance, at least relative, such as the conditions of the moment may involve, and thus to operate a partial recovery, by which the falling movement may appear to be temporarily halted or neutralized[1].

It's easy to understand that these traditional data, of which we must limit ourselves here to a very brief outline, make possible conceptions that are far different from all the attempts at "philosophy of history" that modern people are indulging in, and far more far-reaching and profound. But for the moment, we're not thinking of going back to the origins of the present cycle, or even more simply to the beginnings of *Kali-Yuga*; our intentions relate, in a direct way at least, only to a much more limited domain, to the last phases of this same *Kali-Yuga*. Indeed, within each of the great periods we've been talking about, we can still distinguish various secondary phases, which constitute as many subdivisions; and, each part being in some way analogous to the whole, these subdivisions reproduce, so to speak, on a smaller scale, the general progress of the great cycle into which they are integrated; but, here again, a complete search for the ways in which this law is applied to the various particular cases would take us far beyond the framework we've drawn up for this study. To conclude these preliminary considerations, we'll just mention a few of the last particularly critical periods through which mankind has passed, those that fall within the period we usually call "historical", because it is the only one that is really accessible to ordinary or "profane" history; and this will lead us naturally to the subject of our own study, since the last of these critical periods is none other than that which constitutes what we call modern times.

It's a rather strange fact, which seems never to have been noticed as it deserves to be: it's that the strictly "historical" period, in the sense we've just indicated, goes back exactly to the sixth century before the Christian era, as if there were a barrier in time that couldn't be crossed using the means of investigation available to ordinary researchers. From this period onwards, in fact, we have a fairly precise and well-established chronology everywhere; for anything earlier, on the contrary, we generally obtain only a very vague approximation, and the dates proposed for the same events often vary by several centuries. Even for countries where we have more than just scattered vestiges, like Egypt for example, this is very striking; And what is perhaps even more astonishing is that, in an exceptional and privileged case such as that of China, which possesses, for much more remote periods, annals dated by means of astronomical observations that should leave no room for doubt, moderns nonetheless describe these periods as "legendary", as if this were a domain in which they recognize no right to certainty, and in which they themselves forbid themselves to obtain any. The so-called "classical" antiquity is therefore, to tell the truth, only a relative antiquity, and even much closer to modern times than to true antiquity, since it doesn't even go back to halfway through the *Kali-Yuga*, the duration of which is itself, according to Hindu doctrine, only the tenth part of that of the *Manvantara*; and we can judge from this how far moderns are right to be proud of the extent of their historical knowledge! To justify themselves, they would no doubt reply that these are only "legendary" periods, and that's why they feel they don't need to take them into account; but this answer is precisely an admission of their ignorance, and of a lack of understanding that alone can explain their disdain for tradition; the specifically modern spirit is in fact, as we'll show later, nothing other than the anti-traditional spirit.

In the sixth century before the Christian era considerable changes took place among almost all peoples, whatever the cause, and these changes varied from country to country. In some cases, the tradition was readapted to conditions other than those which had previously existed, and this readaptation was carried out in a rigorously orthodox sense. This was the case in China, where the doctrine, originally constituted as a single whole, was then divided into two clearly distinct parts: Taoism, reserved for an elite, and comprising pure metaphysics and traditional sciences of a strictly speculative nature; Confucianism, common to all without distinction, and having as its domain practical and mainly social applications. The Persians also seem to have readapted Mazdeism, as this was the time of the last Zoroaster[2]. In India, Buddhism was born, which, whatever its original character[3], was to lead, on the contrary, at least in some of its branches, to a revolt against the traditional spirit, going as far as the negation of all authority, to a veritable anarchy, in the etymological sense of "absence of principle", in the intellectual and social order. Curiously enough, there are no monuments in India dating back further than this period, and Orientalists, who want to start with Buddhism (whose importance they singularly exaggerate), have tried to take advantage of this observation to support their thesis: all previous constructions were made of wood, so they naturally disappeared without a trace[4]; but what is true is that such a change in the mode of construction necessarily corresponds to a profound change in the general conditions of existence of the people among whom it occurred.

Closer to the West, we see that the same period was also that of the Babylonian captivity for the Jews; and what is perhaps one of the most astonishing facts we have to note is that a short period of seventy years was enough for them to lose even their writing, since they then had to reconstitute the Sacred Books with characters quite different from those which had been in use until then. We could cite many other events around the same date: we'll just note that this was the beginning of the "historical" period for Rome, following on from the "legendary" era of the kings, and that we also know, albeit vaguely, that there were important movements among the Celtic peoples at this time; but, without dwelling on it further, we'll move on to what concerns Greece. There too, the sixth century was the starting point of the so-called "classical" civilization, the only one that moderns recognize as "historical", and all that precedes is poorly enough known to be treated as "legendary", although recent archaeological discoveries no longer allow us to doubt that, at least, there was a very real civilization there; and we have reason to believe that this first Hellenic civilization was far more intellectually interesting than the one that followed, and that their relationship is not without some analogy to that between medieval and modern Europe. However, it should be noted that the split was not as radical as in the latter case, for there was, at least partially, a readaptation carried out in the traditional order, mainly in the field of the "mysteries" ; and Pythagoreanism, which was above all, in a new form, a restoration of earlier Orphism, and whose obvious links with the Delphic cult of the Hyperborean Apollo even make it possible to envisage a continuous and regular filiation with one of mankind's most ancient traditions. But, on the other hand, we soon saw the emergence of something we had never seen before, and which was to exert a damaging influence on the entire Western world: we're talking about that special mode of thought which took and kept the name of "philosophy"; and this point is important enough for us to dwell on it for a few moments.

Etymologically, the word "philosophy" means nothing other than "love of wisdom"; it therefore designates, first and foremost, a preliminary disposition required to attain wisdom, and it can also, by a natural extension, designate the research which, born of this very disposition, should lead to knowledge. It is therefore only a preliminary and preparatory stage, a progression towards wisdom, a degree corresponding to a state inferior to wisdom[5]; the deviation that subsequently occurred consisted in taking this transitional degree for the goal itself, in claiming to substitute "philosophy" for wisdom, which implies forgetting or misunderstanding the true nature of the latter. This is how what we might call "profane" philosophy came into being, i.e., a purportedly purely human wisdom of a merely rational order, taking the place of true, supra-rational, "non-human" traditional wisdom. Yet something of this wisdom remained throughout antiquity; This is proved first and foremost by the persistence of the "mysteries", whose essentially "initiatory" character cannot be disputed, and also by the fact that the teaching of the philosophers themselves often had both an "exoteric" and an "esoteric" side, the latter allowing for a connection to a higher point of view, as clearly manifested, albeit perhaps incompletely in some respects, a few centuries later by the Alexandrians. For "profane" philosophy to be definitively constituted as such, "exotericism" alone had to remain, and all "esotericism" had to be purely and simply negated; this is precisely what the movement begun by the Greeks was to lead to in modern times; The tendencies that had already asserted themselves among the Greeks were then to be pushed to their most extreme consequences, and the excessive importance they had accorded to rational thought was to be further accentuated, culminating in "rationalism", a particularly modern attitude that consists not even simply in ignoring, but in expressly denying everything of a supra-rational order; but let's not anticipate any further, for we shall have to return to these consequences and see their development in another part of our presentation.

In the light of what has just been said, one thing is particularly important for our purposes: we should look to "classical" antiquity for some of the origins of the modern world. So the modern world is not entirely wrong when it commends itself on Greco-Latin civilization and claims to be its continuator. It has to be said, however, that this is only a distant and somewhat unfaithful continuation, for there were, in spite of everything, many things in this antiquity, in the intellectual and spiritual order, whose equivalent cannot be found in the modern world; they are, in any case, in the progressive obscuration of true knowledge, two quite different degrees. It might be conceivable that the decadence of ancient civilization would have led, gradually and seamlessly, to a state more or less similar to the one we see today; but, in fact, this was not the case, and, in the meantime, there was another critical epoch for the West, which was at the same time one of those periods of recovery to which we referred earlier.

This is the time of the beginning and expansion of Christianity, coinciding, on the one hand, with the dispersion of the Jewish people, and, on the other, with the last phase of Greco-Latin civilization; and we can pass more quickly over these events, in spite of their importance, because they are more generally known than those we have spoken of so far, and their synchronism has been more remarked upon, even by historians whose views are the most superficial. Certain features common to ancient decadence and the present day have also been pointed out often enough; and, without wishing to push the parallelism too far, we must admit that there are indeed some rather striking similarities. Purely "profane" philosophy had gained ground: the emergence of skepticism on the one hand, and the success of Stoic and Epicurean "moralism" on the other, show just how far intellectuality had sunk. At the same time, the old sacred doctrines, which almost no-one understood any more, had degenerated into "paganism" in the true sense of the word, i.e. they were no more than "superstitions", things which, having lost their deeper meaning, survive on themselves through outward manifestations. Hellenism itself tried to revitalize itself with elements borrowed from the Eastern doctrines with which it came into contact. But this was no longer enough: Greco-Latin civilization had to come to an end, and the recovery had to come from elsewhere and take a completely different form. It was Christianity that brought about this transformation; and, let us note in passing, the comparison that can be drawn in certain respects between that time and our own is perhaps one of the determining factors in the disordered "messianism" that is currently emerging. After the troubled period of the barbarian encroachments, necessary to complete the destruction of the old state of things, a normal order was restored for a few centuries; this was the Middle Ages, so misunderstood by modern people who are incapable of understanding its intellectuality, and for whom this period certainly seems much more foreign and remote than "classical" antiquity

For us, the true Middle Ages extend from the reign of Charlemagne to the beginning of the fourteenth century, at which point a new decadence begins which, through various stages, will continue to deepen until the present day. This is the real starting point of the modern crisis: it's the beginning of the disintegration of "Christendom", with which the Western civilization of the Middle Ages was essentially identified; it's also the end of the feudal regime, closely linked to this same "Christendom", and the origin of the constitution of "nationalities". The Renaissance and the Reformation are above all results, and were only made possible by the preceding decadence; but, far from being a recovery, they marked a much deeper fall, because they consummated the definitive break with the traditional spirit, one in the field of science and the arts, the other in the field of religion itself, which was nonetheless the one where such a break might have seemed most difficult to conceive.

Under the pretext of returning to Greco-Roman civilization, we took from it only the most external aspects, because only these could be clearly expressed in written texts. And this incomplete restitution could only have been highly artificial, since it involved forms that had ceased to live their true life centuries ago. As for the traditional sciences of the Middle Ages, after having had a few last manifestations around this time, they disappeared as completely as those of distant civilizations that were once wiped out by some cataclysm; and this time, nothing was to replace them. All that remained was "profane" philosophy and science, the negation of true intellectuality, the limitation of knowledge to the lowest order, the empirical and analytical study of facts that are not linked to any principle, the dispersion into an indefinite multitude of insignificant details, the accumulation of unfounded hypotheses that incessantly destroy each other, and fragmentary views that can lead to nothing except those practical applications that constitute the only effective superiority of modern civilization; An unenviable superiority, moreover, which, by developing to the point of suffocating all other concerns, has given this civilization the purely material character that makes it a veritable monstrosity.

What is quite extraordinary is the speed with which the civilization of the Middle Ages fell into complete oblivion; the men of the seventeenth century no longer had the slightest notion of it, and the surviving monuments no longer represented anything in their eyes, either intellectually or even aesthetically; we can judge from this how much mentality had changed in the meantime. We won't go into the complex factors that contributed to this change, which was so radical that it's hard to believe it could have taken place spontaneously and without the intervention of a guiding force, the exact nature of which necessarily remains rather enigmatic; There are, in this respect, very strange circumstances, such as the popularization, at a given moment, and presenting them as new discoveries, of things which had in reality been known for a very long time, but whose knowledge, because of certain disadvantages which risked outweighing the advantages, had not been spread until then in the public domain[6]. It is equally implausible that the legend which depicts the Middle Ages as a time of "darkness", ignorance and barbarism, should have originated and gained credence of its own accord, and that the veritable falsification of history which moderns have indulged in should have been undertaken without any preconceived ideas; but we shall go no further in examining this question, for, however this work may have been accomplished, it is, for the moment, the observation of the result which, all in all, matters most to us.

There's a word that was given pride of place during the Renaissance, and which summed up the whole program of modern civilization: it's "humanism". In fact, the idea was to reduce everything to purely human proportions, to disregard all principles of a higher order and, symbolically, to turn away from heaven on the pretext of conquering the earth. The Greeks, whose example we claimed to be following, had never gone so far in this direction, even at the time of their greatest intellectual decadence, and at least utilitarian preoccupations had never come to the fore in their case, as was soon to happen with the moderns. Humanism" was already a first form of what has become contemporary "profanism"; and, in seeking to reduce everything to the measure of man, taken as an end in himself, we have ended up descending, step by step, to the level of what is most inferior in man, and by no longer seeking anything more than the satis-faction of the needs inherent in the material side of his nature - a very illusory quest, moreover, since it always creates more artificial needs than it can satisfy.

Will the modern world go all the way down this fatal slope, or, as happened with the decadence of the Greco-Latin world, will a new upturn occur, this time again, before it reaches the bottom of the abyss into which it is being dragged? It would seem that stopping halfway is no longer possible, and that, according to all the indications provided by traditional doctrines, we have truly entered the final phase of the *Kali-Yuga*, the darkest period of this "dark age", a state of dissolution from which it is only possible to emerge by means of a cataclysm, for it is no longer a simple recovery that is then necessary, but a total renovation. Disorder and confusion reign in all domains; they have been brought to a point that far surpasses anything seen before, and, having started in the West, they now threaten to invade the whole world; we are well aware that their triumph can only ever be apparent and fleeting, but, to such a degree, it appears to be the sign of the gravest of all crises that humanity has gone through in its current cycle. Have we not arrived at that dreaded epoch foretold by the sacred books of India, "when castes will be mingled, when the family itself will no longer exist"? We need only look around us to be convinced that this is indeed the state of the world today, and to see everywhere that profound decay which the Gospel calls "the abomination of desolation". We must not hide the serious-ness of the situation; we must see it as it is, without any "op-timism", but also without any "pessimism", since, as we said earlier, the end of the Old World will also be the beginning of a new one.

Now a question arises: what is the raison d'être of a period such as the present? Indeed, however abnormal the present conditions may be considered in themselves, they must nevertheless fit into the general order of things, into that order which, according to an Far Eastern formula, is made up of the sum of all disorders; this epoch, however painful and troubled it may be, must also, like all the others, have its marked place in the whole of human development, and moreover the very fact that it was foreseen by traditional doctrines is a sufficient indication in this respect. What we have said about the general progression of a cycle of manifestation towards progressive materialization provides an immediate explanation for such a state, and shows clearly that what is abnormal and disordered from a particular point of view is merely the consequence of a law relating to a higher or more extensive point of view. We would add, without dwelling on it, that, like any change of state, the passage from one cycle to another can only be accomplished in darkness. This is another very important law, with many applications, but one which, by its very nature, would take us too far to explain in detail[7].

But that's not all: the modern era must necessarily correspond to the development of some of the possibilities which, from the outset, were included in the potentiality of the present cycle; and, however inferior the rank occupied by these possibilities in the hierarchy of the whole, they were nonetheless, as well as the others, to be called into manifestation according to the order assigned to them. In this respect, what tradition tells us characterizes the final phase of the cycle is the exploitation of all that was neglected or rejected during the preceding phases. And this is indeed what we can observe in modern civilization, which in a way lives only on what previous civilizations did not want. To see this, we need only look at how the representatives of those civilizations that have survived in the Eastern world appreciate Western science and its industrial applications. This inferior knowledge, so futile in the eyes of those who possess knowledge of a different order, had to be "realized", and it could only be realized at a stage when true intellectuality had disappeared; this exclusively practical research, in the narrowest sense of the word, had to be carried out, but it could only be done at the opposite extreme from primordial spirituality, by men so immersed in matter that they could conceive of nothing beyond it, and becoming all the more enslaved to it the more they would like to make use of it, leading them to ever-increasing agitation, without rule and without goal, to dispersion in pure multiplicity, until final dissolution.

Such is the true explanation of the modern world, sketched out in broad strokes and reduced to its essentials; but, let us state quite clearly, this explanation can in no way be taken as a justification. An unavoidable misfortune is no less a misfortune; and even if a good comes out of an evil, this does not detract from the evil's character. Of course, we use the terms "good" and "evil" here only to make ourselves clearer, and without any specifically "moral" intention. Partial disorders cannot fail to exist, because they are necessary elements of total order; but, in spite of this, an era of disorder is, in itself, something comparable to a monstrosity, which, while being the consequence of certain natural laws, is nonetheless a deviation and a kind of error, or to a cataclysm, which, while resulting from the normal course of things, is all the same, if we consider it in isolation, an upheaval and an anomaly. Modern civilization, like all things, necessarily has its raison d'être, and if it is truly the end of a cycle, it can be said that it is what it must be, that it comes in its time and its place; but it will nonetheless have to be judged according to the too-often misunderstood Gospel saying: "There must be scandal; but woe to him through whom the scandal comes!"

---

1 - This refers to the function of "divine preservation", which in Hindu tradition is represented by *Vishnu*, and more specifically to the doctrine of the *Avatâras* or "descents" of the divine principle into the manifested world, which we naturally can't think of developing here.

2 - It should be noted that the name Zoroaster in fact designates not a particular person, but a function, both prophetic and legislative; there were several Zoroasters, who lived at very different times; and it is even likely that this function must have had a collective character, in the same way as that of Vyâsa in India, and in the same way as, in Egypt, what was attributed to Thoth or Hermes represents the work of the entire priestly caste.

3 - The question of Buddhism is, in fact, far from being as simple as this brief overview might suggest; and it's interesting to note that, while Hindus, from the point of view of their own tradition, have always condemned Buddhists, many of them nonetheless profess great respect for the Buddha himself, some even going so far as to see in him the ninth Avatâra, while others identify him with Christ. On the other hand, as far as Buddhism as we know it today is concerned, we must be careful to distinguish between its two forms of *Mahâyâna* and *Hinayâna*, or

"Greater Vehicle" and "Lesser Vehicle"; generally spea-king, we can say that Buddhism outside India differs si-gnificantly from its original Indian form, which began to lose ground rapidly after Ashoka's death and disappeared completely a few centuries later.

4 - This case is not peculiar to India, and can also be found in the West; it's for exactly the same reason that no remains can be found of Gallic cities, whose existence is however indisputable, being attested by contemporary testimonies; and, here too, modern historians have taken advantage of this absence of monuments to depict the Gauls as savages living in the forests.

5 - The relationship here is much the same as that which exists, in Taoist doctrine, between the state of "gifted man" and that of "transcendent man".

6 - We'll cite just two examples of facts of this kind that were to have the most serious consequences: the alleged inven-tion of printing, which the Chinese knew about before the Christian era, and the "official" discovery of America, with which communications were much more regular than we think throughout the Middle Ages.

7 - In the Eleusinian mysteries, this law was represented by the symbolism of the grain of wheat; alchemists repre-sented it by "putrefaction" and by the black color that marks the beginning of the "Great Work"; what Christian mystics call the "dark night of the soul" is simply its ap-plication to the spiritual development of the being as it rises to higher states; and it would be easy to point out many other concordances.

CHAPTER II

THE OPPOSITION BETWEEN
EAST AND WEST

One of the particular characteristics of the modern world is the split between East and West; and, although we have already dealt with this question in a more special way, it is necessary to return to it here to clarify certain aspects and dispel certain misunderstandings. The truth is that there have always been diverse and multiple civilizations, each of which has developed in its own way and in accordance with the aptitudes of a particular people or race; but distinction does not mean opposition, and there can be a kind of equivalence between civilizations of very different forms, as long as they are all based on the same fundamental principles, of which they represent only applications conditioned by varied circumstances. This is the case for all civilizations that we can call normal, or traditional; there is no essential opposition between them, and any differences are only external and superficial. On the other hand, a civilization which recognizes no higher principle, which is even founded in reality on a negation of principles, is thereby deprived of any means of agreement with the others, for this agreement, to be truly profound and effective, can only be established from above, that is to say precisely by what this abnormal and deviant civilization lacks. In the present state of the world, we therefore have, on the one hand, all the civilizations that have remained faithful to the traditional spirit, and which are the Eastern civilizations, and, on the other, a civilization that is truly anti-traditional, which is modern Western civilization.

However, some have gone so far as to deny that the very division of humanity into East and West is a reality; but, at least for the present day, this does not seem to be seriously in doubt. Firstly, that there is a Western civilization, common to Europe and America, is a fact on which everyone must agree, whatever judgement one may make on the value of this civilization. As far as the East is concerned, things are less simple, because there is indeed not one, but several Eastern civilizations; but it is enough that they possess certain common traits, those which characterize what we have called a traditional civilization, and that these same traits are not found in Western civilization, for the distinction and even the opposition of East and West to be fully justified. This is indeed the case, and the traditional character is indeed common to all Eastern civilizations, for which we shall recall, in order to better fix ideas, the general division we adopted earlier, and which, although perhaps a little oversimplified if we wanted to go into detail, is nevertheless accurate when we stick to the broad outlines: the Far East, represented essentially by Chinese civilization; the Middle

East, by Hindu civilization; the Near East, by Islamic civilization. It should be added that, in many respects, Islamic civilization should be regarded as an intermediary between the East and the West, and that many of its characteristics even bring it closer to the Western civilization of the Middle Ages; but, if we consider it in relation to the modern West, we must recognize that it is opposed to it in the same way as the civilizations that are properly Eastern, with which it must therefore be associated from this point of view.

The opposition between East and West had no raison d'être when there were also traditional civilizations in the West; it therefore only makes sense in the case of the modern West, because this opposition is much more that of two minds than that of two more or less clearly defined geographical entities. At certain periods, the closest to us being the Middle Ages, the Western mind strongly resembled, in its most important aspects, what the Eastern mind still is today, much more than what it has itself become in modern times; Western civilization was then comparable to Eastern civilizations, in the same way as the latter are to each other. Over the last few centuries, there has been a considerable change, far more serious than any deviation that may have occurred in earlier periods of decadence, since it even goes as far as a veritable reversal in the direction given to human activity; and it is exclusively in the Western world that this change has originated. Consequently, when we say Western spirit, referring to what exists at present, what we mean by this is nothing other than the modern spirit; and, as the other spirit has only been maintained in the East, we can, still in relation to present conditions, call it the Eastern spirit. In short, these two terms express nothing more than a factual situation; and, while it is clear that one of the two spirits is indeed Western, because its appearance belongs to recent history, we do not intend to prejudge the origin of the other, which was once common to East and West, and whose origin, in fact, This is the spirit that could be described as normal, if only because it has inspired all the civilizations we know to a greater or lesser degree, with the exception of one, modern Western civilization.

We have never written anything of the sort, or even anything to suggest such an opinion, for the simple reason that we know very well that it is false. Indeed, it is precisely the traditional data that clearly oppose an assertion of this kind: we find everywhere the formal assertion that the primordial tradition of the present cycle came from the Hyperborean regions; there were then several secondary currents, corresponding to different periods, one of the most important of which, at least among those whose vestiges are still discernible, undoubtedly went from the West to the East. What we are saying is, firstly, that the repository of primordial tradition has long since been transferred to the East, and that it is there that the doctrinal forms most directly derived from it are now to be found; secondly, in the present state of affairs, the true spirit of tradition, with all that it implies, is only authentically represented in the East.

To complete this clarification, we must also explain, at least briefly, certain ideas for the restoration of a "Western tradition" that have emerged in various contemporary circles; their only interest, basically, is to show that some minds are no longer satisfied with modern negation, that they feel the need for something other than what our era offers them, that they see the possibility of a return to tradition, in one form or another, as the only way out of the current crisis. Unfortunately, "traditionalism" is not the same thing as true traditional spirit; it can be, and very often is, no more than a simple tendency, a more or less vague aspiration, which pre-supposes no real knowledge; and, in the mental disarray of our times, this aspiration provokes above all, it must be said, fanciful and chimerical conceptions, devoid of any serious foundation. Finding no authentic tradition on which to rely, people go so far as to imagine pseudo-traditions that never existed, and which are just as lacking in principles as those they would like to replace; all modern disorder is reflected in these constructions, and, whatever the intentions of their authors, the only result they achieve is to make a new con-tribution to the general imbalance. We'll only mention for the record, in this respect, the so-called "Western tradition" fabricated by certain occultists from the most disparate ele-ments, and intended above all to compete with a no less ima-ginary "Eastern tradition", that of the Theosophists; we've said enough about these things elsewhere, and we'd prefer to come straight to the examination of a few other theories that may seem more worthy of attention, because we find in them at least the desire to appeal to traditions that have had an ac-tual existence.

We alluded earlier to the traditional current coming from the western regions; the stories of the ancients, relating to Atlantis, indicate its origin; after the disappearance of this continent, which was the last of the great cataclysms of the past, there seems to be no doubt that remnants of its tradition were transported to various regions, where they mingled with other pre-existing traditions, principally with branches of the great Hyperborean tradition; and it is quite possible that the doctrines of the Celts, in particular, were one of the products of this fusion. We're far from disputing this, but let's keep one thing in mind: the "Atlantean" form itself disappeared thousands of ago, along with the civilization to which it belonged, and whose destruction can only have been the result of a deviation that was perhaps comparable, in some respects, to the one we see today, albeit with a notable difference in that humanity had not yet entered the *Kali-Yuga*; it's also that this tradition corresponded only to a secondary period of our cycle, and that it would be a great mistake to claim to identify it with the primordial tradition from which all the others stem, and which alone remains from beginning to end. It would be out of place here to set out all the data justifying these assertions; we will only draw the conclusion that it is impossible to revive an "Atlantean" tradition at present, or even to relate to it more or less directly; indeed, there is much fantasy in attempts of this kind. It is nevertheless true that it can be interesting to research the origin of elements found in later traditions, provided we do so with all the precautions necessary to avoid certain illusions; but such research can in no way lead to the resurrection of a tradition that would not be adapted to any of our world's current conditions.

There are others who want to link up with "Celticism", and because they are appealing to something less distant from us, it may seem that what they are proposing is less impractical; yet where will they find "Celticism" today in its purest state, and still endowed with sufficient vitality for it to be possible to take support from it? We're not talking about archaeological or simply "literary" reconstructions, as we've seen a few; we're talking about something quite different. It's true that highly recognizable and still usable Celtic elements have come down to us through various intermediaries; but these elements are a long way from representing the entirety of a tradition, and, surprisingly, in the very countries where it once lived, it is now even more completely ignored than those of many civilizations that were always foreign to these same countries; isn't this something that should give pause for thought, at least to those who are not entirely dominated by a preconceived idea? We'd say more: in all cases like this, where we're dealing with the vestiges left by vanished civilizations, it's only possible to truly understand them by comparison with what's similar in traditional civilizations that are still alive; and the same can be said for the Middle Ages themselves, where we encounter so many things whose meaning is lost to modern Westerners. This contact with traditions whose spirit still survives is even the only way to revive what is still susceptible of being revived; and this, as we have already indicated many times, is one of the greatest services that the East can render to the West. We do not deny the survival of a certain "Celtic spirit", which can still manifest itself in various forms, as it has done at different times; but when we are assured that there are still spiritual centers that fully preserve the Druidic tradition, we expect to be provided with proof, and until further notice, this seems highly doubtful, if not totally implausible.

The truth is that the surviving Celtic elements were, for the most part, assimilated by Christianity in the Middle Ages; the legend of the "Holy Grail", with all that goes with it, is a particularly convincing and significant example of this. We believe, moreover, that a Western tradition, if it managed to reconstitute itself, would necessarily take an outwardly religious form, in the strictest sense of the word, and that this form could only be Christian, for, on the one hand, other possible forms have been alien to the Western mentality for too long, and, on the other hand, it is in Christianity alone, let's say more precisely in Catholicism, that the remnants of traditional spirit that still survive in the West are to be found. Any "traditionalist" attempt that fails to take this fact into account is inevitably doomed to failure, because it lacks a basis; it is all too obvious that one can only rely on what actually exists, and that, where continuity is lacking, there can only be artificial reconstitutions that cannot be viable; If it is objected that Christianity itself, in our time, is no longer truly understood in its deepest sense, we would reply that it has at least retained, in its very form, all that is necessary to provide the basis of the question at hand. The least fanciful attempt, the only one that does not run up against immediate impossibilities, would therefore be to restore something comparable to what existed in the Middle Ages, with the differences required by changed circumstances; and, for all that is entirely lost in the West, it would be advisable to call on the traditions that have been preserved in their entirety, as we indicated earlier, and then to carry out a work of adaptation that could only be the work of a strongly constituted intellectual elite. We've already said all this, but it's worth stressing it again, because there's too much inconsistent daydreaming going on at the moment, and also because it's important to understand that, while Eastern traditions, in their proper forms, can certainly be assimilated by an elite which, by definition, must in some way be beyond all forms, they can probably never be assimilated, barring unforeseen transformations, by the generality of Westerners, for whom they were not made. If a Western elite can be formed, true knowledge of Eastern doctrines, for the reason we have just indicated, will be indispensable to it in fulfilling its function; but those who will only have to reap the benefits of its work, and who will be the greatest number, may well have no awareness of these things, and the influence they will receive from them, as it were without suspecting it and in any case by means that will entirely escape them, will be no less real or effective for that. We've never said anything else, but we feel we should repeat it here as clearly as possible, because if we can't always expect to be fully understood by everyone, we at least want to be sure that people don't attribute to us intentions that are in no way our own.

But let's leave all anticipations aside, since it's the present state of affairs that should concern us most, and return for a moment to the ideas of restoring a "Western tradition", as we can observe them around us. A single remark will suffice to show that these ideas are not "in order", if we may put it that way: they are almost always conceived in a spirit of more or less avowed hostility towards the East. It must be said that even those who would like to base their arguments on Christianity are sometimes animated by this spirit; they seem to seek above all to discover oppositions which, in reality, are perfectly non-existent; and it is thus that we have heard the absurd opinion put forward that, although the same things are found both in Christianity and in Eastern doctrines, and expressed on both sides in an almost identical form, they do not however have the same meaning in the two cases, that they even have an opposite meaning! Those who make such assertions prove that, whatever their claims, they have not gone very far in understanding traditional doctrines, since they have not glimpsed the fundamental identity that lies hidden beneath all the differences in outward form, and even where this identity becomes quite apparent, they still persist in ignoring it.

This is the principle they lack, in which they are affected, far more than they can imagine, by the modern spirit against which they would like to react; and, when they use the word "tradition", they certainly don't mean it in the same way as we do.

In the mental confusion that characterizes our times, we have come to apply the same word "tradition" indiscriminately to all sorts of things, often quite insignificant, such as simple customs of no significance at all, and sometimes of very recent origin; we have reported elsewhere a similar abuse of the word "religion". We must be wary of these deviations of language, which reflect a kind of degeneration of the corresponding ideas; and just because someone calls himself a "traditionalist" doesn't mean he knows, however imperfectly, what tradition is in the true sense of the word. For our part, we absolutely refuse to give this name to anything of a purely human nature; it's not inappropriate to state this expressly when we constantly come across, for example, an expression like "traditional philosophy". A philosophy, even if it really is all it can be, has no right to this title, because it is entirely within the rational order, even if it does not deny what goes beyond it, and because it is only a construction built by human individuals, without revelation or inspiration of any kind, or, to sum it all up in a single word, because it is something essentially "profane". What's more, despite all the illusions in which some people seem to indulge, it's certainly not a science that's all "books" that can suffice to straighten out the mentality of a race and an era; and for that you need something other than philosophical speculation, which, even in the most favorable case, is condemned by its very nature to remain entirely external and much more verbal than real. To restore the lost tradition, to truly revitalize it, we need contact with the living traditional spirit, and, as we've already said, it's only in the East that this spirit is still fully alive; it's no less true that this presupposes above all, in the West, an aspiration towards a return to this traditional spirit, but it can hardly be anything more than a simple aspiration. The few movements of "anti-modern" reaction that have taken place so far - incomplete, in our opinion - can only confirm us in this conviction, for all this, which is undoubtedly excellent in its negative and critical part, is nevertheless far removed from a restoration of true intellectuality, and develops only within the limits of a rather restricted mental horizon. It is something, however, in the sense that it is indicative of a state of mind that would have been hard to find the slightest trace of only a few years ago; if all Westerners are no longer unanimous in being content with the exclusively material development of modern civilization, this is perhaps a sign that, for them, all hope of salvation is not yet entirely lost.

Be that as it may, if we suppose that the West were in any way to return to its tradition, its opposition to the East would be resolved and would cease to exist, since it only came into being as a result of Western deviation, and is in reality nothing more than the opposition of the traditional spirit and the anti-traditional spirit. So, contrary to the assumption of those we alluded to a moment ago, one of the first results of a return to tradition would be to make an understanding with the East immediately possible, as it is between all civilizations that possess comparable or equivalent elements, and only between those, for it is these elements that constitute the only ground on which such an understanding can validly take place. The true traditional spirit, whatever form it takes, is everywhere and always the same at heart; the various forms, which are specially adapted to such and such mental conditions, to such and such circumstances of time and place, are but expressions of one and the same truth; but one must be able to place oneself in the order of pure intellectuality to discover this fundamental unity beneath their apparent multiplicity. Moreover, it is in this intellectual order that reside the principles on which all the rest normally depend as consequences or more or less remote applications; it is therefore on these principles that we must first agree, if we are to have a truly profound understanding, since this is what is essential; and, once we really understand them, agreement is self-evident. It should be noted, in fact, that knowledge of principles, which is knowledge par excellence, metaphysical knowledge in the true sense of the word, is as universal as the principles themselves, and therefore entirely free of all individual contingencies, which on the contrary necessarily come into play as soon as we come to the applications; so this purely intellectual domain is the only one where there is no need for an effort of adaptation between different mentalities. What's more, once work of this kind has been accomplished, all that's left to do is to develop the results, so that agreement in all other fields is also achieved, since, as we've just said, this is what everything directly or indirectly depends on; on the other hand, agreement reached in a particular field, apart from principles, will always be eminently unstable and precarious, and much more like a diplomatic combination than a genuine agreement. And this must be understood in a double sense: we must start from the highest, i.e. principles, and gradually work down to the various orders of application, always rigorously observing the hierarchical dependence that exists between them; and this work, by its very nature, can only be that of an elite, giving this word its truest and most complete meaning: It is an intellectual elite that we wish to speak of exclusively, and, in our eyes, there can be no other, all external social distinctions being of no importance from our point of view.

In fact, the two questions are so closely linked that they are one and the same, and we have just given the reasons why this is so. We will now have to show more fully what the anti-traditional spirit, which is properly the modern spirit, consists of, and what consequences it carries within itself, consequences which we see unfolding with ruthless logic in current events; but before we come to that, one last thought is in order. To be resolutely "anti-modern" is not to be "anti-Western", if we can use that word, since it is, on the contrary, to make the only valid effort to try to save the West from its own disorder; and, on the other hand, no Oriental faithful to his own tradition can see things any differently than we do ourselves; there are certainly far fewer opponents of the West as such, which would make little sense, than of the West insofar as it identifies itself with modern civilization. Some today speak of "defending the West", which is truly singular, when, as we shall see later, it is the West that threatens to overwhelm everything and drag the whole of humanity into the whirlpool of its disordered activity; singular, we say, and totally unjustified, if they intend, as it seems, despite a few restrictions, that this defense should be directed against the East, for the true East has no intention of attacking or dominating anyone, and asks for nothing more than its independence and tranquillity, which, we agree, is quite legitimate. The truth, however, is that the West is indeed in great need of defense, but only against itself, against its own tendencies which, if pushed to the limit, will inevitably lead it to ruin and destruction; it is therefore "reform of the West" that should be said, and this reform, if it were what it should be, i.e. a true traditional restoration, would have as its very natural consequence a rapprochement with the East. For our part, we would like nothing more than to contribute, within the limits of our means, to both this reform and this rapprochement, if there is still time, and if such a result can be obtained before the final catastrophe towards which modern civilization is marching with great strides; But even if it were already too late to avert this catastrophe, the work accomplished with this intention would not be useless, for it would in any case serve to prepare, however distantly, this "discrimination" of which we spoke at the beginning, and thus ensure the preservation of those elements which must escape the shipwreck of the present world to become the seeds of the future world.

CHAPTER III

KNOWLEDGE AND ACTION

We will now consider, in a more specific way, one of the main aspects of the opposition that currently exists between the Eastern mind and the Western mind, and which is, more generally, that of the traditional mind and the anti-traditional mind, as we have explained. From a certain point of view, which is one of the most fundamental, this opposition appears to be that of contemplation and action, or, to put it more accurately, that of the respective places to be assigned to each of these two terms. In their relationship, they can be considered in several different ways: are they really two opposites, as is often thought, or are they not rather two complements, or is there not in fact a relationship between them, not of coordination, but of subordination ? Such are the different aspects of the question, and these aspects relate to as many points of view, of very unequal importance moreover, but each of which can be justified in certain respects and corresponds to a certain order of reality.

First of all, the most superficial, the most external of all, is the point of view that consists in purely and simply opposing contemplation and action, as two opposites in the literal sense of the word. And yet, if this opposition were absolutely irreducible, there would be a complete incompatibility between contemplation and action, which could never be brought together. In fact, this is not the case: there is no people, at least in normal cases, and perhaps not even an individual, who can be exclusively contemplative or exclusively active. What is true is that there are two tendencies, one or the other of which almost necessarily dominates, so that the development of one seems to be to the detriment of the other, for the simple reason that human activity, understood in its most general sense, cannot be exercised equally and at the same time in all fields and in all directions. This is what gives the appearance of an opposition; but there must be a possible conciliation between these opposites, or so-called opposites; and, incidentally, the same could be said of all opposites, which cease to be such as soon as, in order to consider them, we rise above a certain level, that at which their opposition has its full reality. Opposition and contrast mean disharmony and imbalance, in other words, something which, as we have already made clear, can only exist from a relative, particular and limited point of view.

By considering contemplation and action as complementary, we're already at a deeper and truer point of view than the previous one, because the opposition is reconciled and resolved, its two terms somehow balancing each other out. It would seem, then, that we are dealing with two equally necessary elements, which complement and support each other, and which constitute the dual activity, inner and outer, of one and the same being, be it each individual man or humanity as a whole. This conception is certainly more harmonious and satisfying than the first; however, if we were to adhere exclusively to it, we would be tempted, by virtue of the correlation thus established, to place contemplation and action on the same plane, so that we would only have to strive to keep the scales as equal as possible between them, without ever raising the question of any superiority of one over the other; and what clearly shows that such a point of view is still insufficient, is that this question of superiority does in fact arise, and always has, whatever the direction in which we wanted to resolve it.

The important question here, moreover, is not one of de facto predominance, which is, after all, a matter of temperament or race, but of what we might call de jure predominance; and the two things are linked only up to a point. Undoubtedly, the recognition of the superiority of one of the two tendencies will encourage us to develop it as much as possible, in preference to the other; but, in application, it is no less true that the place held by contemplation and action in the overall life of a man or a people will always be largely the result of their own nature, for we must take into account the particular possibilities of each one. It is obvious that the capacity for contemplation is more widespread and more generally developed among Orientals; there is probably no country where it is more so than in India, and this is why India can be considered as representing par excellence what we have called the Oriental spirit. On the other hand, it is indisputable that, generally speaking, the aptitude for action, or the tendency resulting from this aptitude, is what predominates among Western peoples, as far as the great majority of individuals are concerned, and that, even if this tendency were not exaggerated and deviated from as it is at present, it would nevertheless remain, so that contemplation could only ever be the concern of a much more restricted elite; This is why it is often said in India that, if the West returned to a normal state and possessed a regular social organization, there would undoubtedly be many *Kshatriyas*, but few *Brahmins*[1]. This would be enough, however, if the intellectual elite were effectively constituted and if its supremacy were recognized, for everything to return to order, for spiritual power is by no means based on numbers, whose law is that of matter; Moreover, it should be noted that in antiquity, and especially in the Middle Ages, Westerners' natural disposition to action did not prevent them from recognizing the superiority of contemplation, i.e. of pure intelligence; why is it different in modern times? Is it because Westerners, by overdeveloping their faculties for action, have come to lose their intellectuality, that they have, to console themselves, invented theories that place action above all else, and even go so far as to deny that anything of value exists outside of it, such as "pragmatism", or is it on the contrary this way of seeing that, having prevailed at first, has brought about the intellectual atrophy we see today? In both hypotheses, and also in the rather probable case where the truth lies in a combination of the one and the other, the results are exactly the same; at the point things have reached, it's high time to react, and it's here, let's say it once again, that the East can come to the rescue of the West, if the latter so wishes, not to impose conceptions that are foreign to it, as some seem to fear, but to help it rediscover its own tradition, the meaning of which it has lost.

We could say that the antithesis of East and West, in the present state of things, consists in the fact that the East maintains the superiority of contemplation over action, while the modern West asserts the superiority of action over contemplation. Here, it's no longer a question of opposition or complementarism, as it was when we were simply talking about a relationship of coordination between the two terms in question; a relationship of subordination being irreversible by its very nature, the two conceptions are really contradictory, and therefore mutually exclusive, so that as soon as we admit that there is indeed subordination, one is necessarily true and the other false. Before getting to the heart of the matter, let's note that, while the spirit that has been maintained in the East is truly of all times, as we said above, the other spirit has only appeared in very recent times, which, apart from any other consideration, may already suggest that it is something abnormal. This impression is confirmed by the very exaggeration to which the modern Western mind, following its own tendency, has fallen. Not content with proclaiming the superiority of action on every occasion, it has come to make action its exclusive preoccupation, and to deny all value to contemplation, whose true nature it either ignores or completely misunderstands. On the contrary, Eastern doctrines, while affirming as clearly as possible the superiority and even transcendence of contemplation over action, nonetheless accord the latter its rightful place and readily acknowledge its full importance in the order of human contingencies[2].

Eastern doctrines, as well as ancient Western ones, are unanimous in affirming that contemplation is superior to action, just as the immutable is superior to change[3]. Action, being but a transitory and momentary modification of being, cannot have in itself its principle and its sufficient reason; if it is not attached to a principle which is beyond its contingent domain, it is but a pure illusion ; And this principle, from which it derives all the reality of which it is susceptible, and its very existence and possibility, can only be found in contemplation or, if one prefers, in knowledge, for these two terms are basically synonymous, or at least coincide, since knowledge itself and the operation by which it is attained cannot in any way be separated[4]. Similarly, change, in its most general sense, is unintelligible and contradictory, i.e. impossible, without a principle from which it proceeds and which, by virtue of being its principle, cannot be subjected to it, and is therefore necessarily immutable; and this is why, in Western antiquity, Aristotle asserted the necessity of the "immovable motor" of all things. Knowledge plays this role precisely in relation to action; it is clear that action belongs entirely to the world of change, of "becoming"; knowledge alone enables us to escape from this world and its inherent limitations, and when it reaches the immutable, as is the case with principial or metaphysical knowledge, which is knowledge par excellence, it itself possesses immutability, for all true knowledge is essentially identification with its object. This is precisely what is ignored by modern Westerners, who have come to regard knowledge only as rational and discursive, i.e. indirect and imperfect, what we might call knowledge by reflection, and who even increasingly appreciate this inferior knowledge only insofar as it can be used immediately for practical purposes; Engaged in action to the point of denying all that goes beyond it, they fail to realize that this very action degenerates, through lack of principle, into agitation as vain as it is sterile.

This is, in fact, the most visible character of the modern age: the need for incessant agitation, continual change, ever-increasing speed like that with which events themselves unfold. It's dispersion in multiplicity, and in a multiplicity that is no longer unified by the awareness of any higher principle; it's, in everyday life as in scientific conceptions, analysis pushed to the extreme, indefinite fragmentation, a veritable disintegration of human activity in all the orders in which it can still be exercised; and hence the ineptitude for synthesis, the impossibility of any concentration, so striking to Eastern eyes. These are the natural and inevitable consequences of ever-increasing materialization, for matter is essentially multiplicity and division, and that's why, let's say it in passing, everything that proceeds from it can only engender struggles and conflicts of all kinds, between peoples as well as individuals. The deeper we go into matter, the more the elements of division and opposition become accentuated and amplified; conversely, the higher we rise towards pure spirituality, the closer we come to unity, which can only be fully realized through awareness of universal principles.

The strangest thing is that movement and change are really sought after for their own sake, and not with a view to any goal to which they may lead; and this fact results directly from the absorption of all human faculties by external action, the momentary nature of which we pointed out earlier. It is dispersion seen in another light, and at a more accentuated stage: it is, we might say, like a tendency towards instantaneity, having as its limit a state of pure imbalance, which, if it could be reached, would coincide with the final dissolution of this world; and it is still one of the clearest signs of the last period of the *Kali-Yuga*.

In this respect, too, the same thing is happening in science: it's research for research's sake, much more so than for the partial and fragmentary results it leads to; it's the increasingly rapid succession of unfounded theories and hypotheses, which, as soon as they've been built up, crumble, to be replaced by others that will last even less, a veritable chaos in the midst of which it would be futile to look for any definitively acquired elements, other than a monstrous accumulation of facts and details that can neither prove nor signify anything. We're talking here, of course, about the speculative point of view, insofar as it still exists ; as far as practical applications are concerned, on the contrary, there are undeniable results, and this is easy to understand, since these applications relate immediately to the material field, and this is precisely the only field in which modern man can boast real superiority. We can therefore expect that mechanical and industrial discoveries, or rather inventions, will continue to develop and multiply, at an ever-increasing pace, right up to the end of the present age; and who knows whether, with the dangers of destruction they themselves carry, they will not be one of the main agents of the ultimate catastrophe, if things come to such a point that it cannot be avoided?

But while a few people sense the danger and try to react, most of our contemporaries revel in this disorder, which they see as an externalized image of their own mentality. There is, in fact, an exact correspondence between a world where everything seems to be in pure "becoming", where there is no longer any place for the immutable and the permanent, and the state of mind of men who make all reality consist in this same "becoming", which implies the negation of true knowledge, as well as of the very object of this knowledge, we mean transcendent and universal principles. We can go even further: it is the negation of all real knowledge, in any order whatsoever, even in the relative, since, as we pointed out above, the relative is unintelligible and impossible without the absolute, the contingent without the necessary, change without the immutable, multiplicity without unity ; relativism" encloses a contradiction within itself, and when we want to reduce everything to change, we should logically end up denying the very existence of change; in fact, Zeno of Elea's famous arguments had no other meaning. It has to be said, in fact, that theories of the kind we're talking about are not exclusively peculiar to modern times, for nothing should be exaggerated; some examples can be found in Greek philosophy, and the case of Heraclitus, with his "universal flow", is the best known in this respect; it is even what led the Eleates to combat these conceptions, as well as those of the atomists, by a kind of reductio ad absurdum. In India itself, something comparable was encountered, but of course from a different point of view than that of philosophy; certain Buddhist schools, in fact, also presented the same character, for one of their main theses was that of the "dissolubility of all things[5]". However, these theories were only exceptions at the time, and such revolts against the traditional mind, which may have occurred throughout the *Kali-Yuga* period, were limited in scope; what is new is the generalization of similar conceptions, as we see in the contemporary West.

It should also be noted that "philosophies of becoming", under the influence of the very recent idea of "progress", have taken on a special form among moderns, which theories of the same kind never had among the ancients: this form, which is moreover susceptible to multiple varieties, is what we can generally designate by the name of "evolutionism". We won't go back over what we've already said elsewhere on this subject; we'll just point out that any conception that admits of nothing other than "becoming" is necessarily, by that very fact, a " naturalistic" conception, implying as such a formal negation of what lies beyond nature, i.e. of the metaphysical realm, which is the realm of immutable and eternal principles. We should also point out, in connection with these anti-metaphysical theories, that Bergson's idea of "pure duration" corresponds exactly to the dispersal into the instantaneous we spoke of earlier; the so-called intuition that models itself on the incessant flow of sensible things, far from being the means of true knowledge, actually represents the dissolution of all possible knowledge.

This leads us to reiterate once again - for this is an absolutely essential point, and one on which it is vital to leave no room for equivocation - that intellectual intuition, through which alone true metaphysical knowledge is obtained, has absolutely nothing in common with that other intuition spoken of by some contemporary philosophers: the latter is of the sensible order, and is properly infra-rational, while the other, which is pure intelligence, is on the contrary supra-rational. But modern people, who know nothing superior to reason in the order of intelligence, cannot even conceive of what intellectual intuition can be, whereas the doctrines of antiquity and the Middle Ages, even when they were merely philosophical in character and therefore could not actually appeal to this intuition, nevertheless expressly recognized its existence and supremacy over all other faculties. That's why there was no such thing as "rationalism" before Descartes; this too is a specifically modern thing, and is closely linked to "individualism", since it is nothing other than the negation of all supra- individual faculties. As long as Westerners persist in ignoring or denying intellectual intuition, they will have no tradition in the true sense of the word, nor will they be able to come to terms with the authentic representatives of Eastern civilizations, in which everything seems to hang on this intuition, unchanging and infallible in itself, and the sole point of departure for all development in line with traditional standards.

1 - Contemplation and action, in fact, are respectively the proper functions of the first two castes, that of the *Brahmins* and that of the *Kshatriyas*; their relationship is also that of spiritual authority and temporal power; but we do not propose to consider this side of the question here, which deserves to be dealt with separately.

2 - Those who doubt the very real, albeit relative, importance of action in traditional Eastern doctrines, particularly in India, need look no further than the *Bhagavad-Gîtâ*, which, it should be remembered, is a book specially designed for *Kshatriyas*.

3 - It is by virtue of the relationship thus established that it is said that the *Brahmin* is the type of stable beings, and that the *Kshatriya* is the type of mobile or changing beings; thus, all beings in this world, according to their nature, are principally related to one or the other, for there is a perfect correspondence between the cosmic order and the human order.

4 - Indeed, as a consequence of the essentially momentary nature of action, it should be noted that, in the realm of action, results are always separate from what produces them, whereas knowledge, on the contrary, bears its fruit within itself.

5 - Soon after its origin, Buddhism in India became associated with one of the main manifestations of the *Kshatriya* revolt against the authority of the *Brahmins* ; and, as is easy to understand from the foregoing indications, there is, generally speaking, a very direct link between the denial of any immutable principle and that of spiritual authority, between the reduction of all reality to "becoming" and the affirmation of the supremacy of temporal power, whose proper domain is the world of action; and we can see that the emergence of "naturalist" or anti-metaphysical doctrines always occurs when the element representing temporal power in a civilization takes precedence over that representing spiritual authority.

CHAPTER IV

SACRED AND PROFANE SCIENCE

In other words, it is pure metaphysical doctrine that constitutes the essential, and everything else is linked to it by way of consequences or applications to the various orders of contingent realities. This is particularly true of social institutions; and, on the other hand, the same is also true of the sciences, i.e. knowledge pertaining to the realm of the relative, and which, in such civilizations, can only be considered as mere dependencies and, as it were, extensions or reflections of absolute and principial knowledge. Thus, the true hierarchy is everywhere and always observed: the relative is not held to be non-existent, which would be absurd; it is taken into consideration insofar as it deserves to be, but it is put in its rightful place, which can only be a secondary and subordinate place; and, within this relative itself, there are very different degrees, depending on whether things are more or less distant from the realm of principles.

We have often alluded to the "traditional sciences" of antiquity and the Middle Ages, which still exist in the East, but the very idea of which is totally foreign to Westerners today. It should be added that each civilization has had its own particular type of "traditional science", because here, we are no longer dealing with universal principles, to which pure metaphysics alone relates, but with adaptations, where, because it is a contingent domain, we must take into account the mental and other conditions of a given people, and even of a given period of that people's existence, since we saw above that there are times when "readaptations" become necessary. These "readaptations" are merely changes of form, which in no way affect the very essence of the tradition; for metaphysical doctrine, expression alone can be modified, in a way that is rather comparable to translating from one language into another; whatever forms it wraps itself in to express itself insofar as this is possible, there is absolutely only one metaphysics, just as there is only one truth. But when we move on to applications, the case is naturally different: with the sciences, as well as with social institutions, we are in the world of form and multiplicity; which is why we can say that other forms truly constitute other sciences, even if they have, at least partially, the same object. Logicians are in the habit of regarding a science as entirely defined by its object, which is inaccurate by oversimplification; the point of view from which this object is viewed must also enter into the definition of the science. There is an indefinite multitude of possible sciences; it may happen that several sciences study the same things, but under such different aspects, and therefore by such different methods and with such different intentions, that they are nonetheless truly distinct sciences. This is particularly true of the "traditional sciences" of different civilizations, which, although comparable, cannot always be assimilated to one another, and often could only be misleadingly referred to by the same names. It goes without saying that the difference is even greater if, instead of drawing a comparison between "traditional sciences", which at least all have the same fundamental character, we want to compare these sciences, in a general way, to the sciences as moderns conceive them; at first sight, it may sometimes seem that the object is the same on both sides, and yet the knowledge that the two kinds of sciences give respectively of this object is so different, that one hesitates, after further examination, to assert identity even in a certain respect only.

First of all, we'll take a very broad example, that of "physics" as understood by the ancients and the moderns. In this case, , there's no need to go outside the Western world to see the profound difference between the two conceptions. The term "physics", in its original and etymological sense, means nothing other than "the science of nature", without any restrictions whatsoever; it is therefore the science that concerns the most general laws of "becoming", because "nature" and "becoming" are basically synonymous, and this is how the Greeks, and Aristotle in particular, understood it; if there are more particular sciences relating to the same order, then they are merely "specifications" of physics for this or that more narrowly defined domain. So there is already something quite significant in the deviation that moderns have made of the word "physics", using it exclusively to designate a particular science among other sciences, all of which are also sciences of nature; This fact is linked to the fragmentation we have already mentioned as one of the characteristics of modern science, to the "specialization" engendered by the spirit of analysis, and pushed to the point of rendering truly inconceivable, for those under its influence, a science dealing with nature considered as a whole. Some of the disadvantages of this "specialization" have often been pointed out, especially the narrowness of vision that is its inevitable consequence; but it seems that even those who were most clearly aware of it resigned themselves to seeing it as a necessary evil, due to the accumulation of detailed knowledge that no man can embrace at a single glance; they have not understood, on the one hand, that this detailed knowledge is insignificant in itself, and is not worth sacrificing to it a synthetic knowledge which, even if still limited to the relative, is of a much higher order, and, on the other hand, that the impossibility of unifying their multiplicity stems solely from the fact that we have refrained from relating them to a higher principle, from the fact that we have stubbornly proceeded from below and from the outside, whereas it would have been necessary to do just the opposite in order to have a science with real speculative value.

If we want to compare ancient physics, not with what moderns call the same word, but with the whole of the natural sciences as they are currently constituted - because that's what they should really correspond to - then we should note, as a first difference, the division into multiple "specialties" that are, so to speak, foreign to each other. However, this is only the most external aspect of the question, and we shouldn't think that, by bringing all these special sciences together, we'd obtain an equivalent of the old physics. The truth is that the point of view is quite different, and it is here that we see the essential difference between the two conceptions we spoke of earlier: the traditional conception, as we said, links all the sciences to principles as so many particular applications, and it is this link that the modern conception does not accept. For Aristotle, physics was only "second" to metaphysics, that is to say, it was dependent on it, and was basically no more than an application, to the realm of nature, of principles superior to nature and reflected in its laws; and the same can be said of the "cosmology" of the Middle Ages. The modern conception, on the other hand, claims to make the sciences independent, by denying everything that goes beyond them, or at least by declaring it "unknowable" and refusing to take it into account, which still amounts to denying it practically; this denial existed in fact long before anyone thought of setting it up as a systematic theory under names such as "positivism" and "agnosticism", for it can be said to be truly at the starting point of all modern science. However, it was only in the nineteenth century that we saw men taking pride in their ignorance, for to proclaim oneself an "agnostic" is nothing other than that, and to claim to forbid everyone to know what they themselves did not know; and this marked a further step in the intellectual decline of the West.

By seeking to radically separate the sciences from any higher principle, on the pretext of ensuring their independence, the modern conception deprives them of any profound meaning or even any real interest from the point of view of knowledge, and can only lead to a dead end, since it confines them to an irremediably limited domain[1]. The development that takes place within this domain is not, moreover, a deepening as some people imagine; on the contrary, it remains entirely superficial, and consists only of that dispersion into detail that we have already pointed out, in an analysis that is as sterile as it is painful, and which can continue indefinitely without advancing a single step along the road to true knowledge. It has to be said, then, that Westerners in general do not cultivate science for its own sake: What they have in mind above all is not knowledge, even inferior knowledge, but practical applications, and to be convinced that this is indeed the case, we need only look at how easily most of our contemporaries confuse science with industry, and how many see the engineer as the very type of scientist; but this relates to another question, which we shall deal with more fully later.

By establishing itself in the modern way, science has not only lost in depth, but also, one might say, in solidity, for its attachment to principles meant that it shared in their immutability to the full extent that its very object allowed, whereas, enclosed exclusively in the world of change, it no longer finds anything stable, any fixed point on which it can rely; No longer starting from any absolute certainty, it is reduced to probabilities and approximations, or to purely hypothetical constructions that are no more than the work of individual fantasy. So, even if modern science happens accidentally to arrive, by a very roundabout route, at certain results that seem to agree with some of the data of the ancient "traditional sciences", it would be a great mistake to see in them a confirmation that these data have no need of; and it would be a waste of time to try to reconcile totally different points of view, or to establish a concordance with hypothetical theories that will perhaps find themselves entirely discredited in a few years' time[2]. For today's science, the things in question can only belong to the realm of hypotheses, whereas for the "traditional sciences", they were something quite different, presented as the indubitable consequences of truths known intuitively, and therefore infallibly, in the metaphysical order[3]. It is, moreover, a singular illusion of modern "experimentalism" to believe that a theory can be proved by the facts, when in reality the same facts can always be explained equally well by several different theories, and that some of the promoters of the experimental method, like Claude Bernard, themselves recognized that they could only interpret them with the help of "preconceived ideas", without which these facts would remain "brute facts", devoid of any meaning or scientific value.

Now that we've come to talk about "experimentalism", we should take the opportunity to answer a question that may arise in this connection, which is: why have the purely experimental sciences received a development in modern civilization that they have never had in other civilizations? It's because these sciences are those of the sensible world, those of matter, and it's also because they are those which give rise to the most immediate practical applications; their development, accompanied by what we would readily call the "superstition of fact", therefore corresponds well to specifically modern tendencies, whereas, on the other hand, previous eras were unable to find sufficient grounds for interest in them to become so attached to them as to neglect knowledge of a higher order. What is illegitimate is only the abuse that occurs when things of this kind absorb all human activity, as we are seeing today. It might even be conceivable that, in a normal civilization, sciences constituted by an experimental method could, as well as others, be linked to principles and thus endowed with a real speculative value; In fact, if this case does not seem to have arisen, it's because attention has preferably been focused elsewhere, and also because, even when it was a question of studying the sensible world to the extent that it might appear interesting to do so, traditional data made it possible to undertake this study more favorably by other methods and from another point of view.

We said earlier that one of the characteristics of the present age is the exploitation of everything that had been neglected until then as being of too secondary importance for men to devote their activity to, and which nevertheless also had to be developed before the end of this cycle, since these things had their place among the possibilities that were called upon to manifest; this is precisely the case, in particular, of the experimental sciences that have come into being in recent centuries. There are even certain modern sciences which, in the most literal sense, truly represent the "residues" of ancient sciences, now misunderstood: it is the most inferior part of the latter which, isolated and detached from all the rest in a period of decadence, was crudely materialized, and then served as the starting point for a completely different development, in a direction consistent with modern trends, so as to result in the constitution of sciences which really have nothing in common with those which preceded them. So, for example, it is wrong to say, as is usually the case, that astrology and alchemy became modern astronomy and chemistry respectively, although there is a certain amount of truth in this opinion from a purely historical point of view, which is exactly what we have just indicated: if the latter of these sciences do indeed proceed from the former in a certain sense, it is not by "evolution" or "progress" as is claimed, but on the contrary by degeneration; and this calls for a few more explanations.

It should be noted, first of all, that the attribution of distinct meanings to the terms "astrology" and "astronomy" is relatively recent; among the Greeks, these two words were used indifferently to designate the whole of what both now apply to. At first glance, therefore, it would seem that we are still dealing here with one of those divisions by "specialization" that were established between what were originally only parts of a single science; but what is peculiar here is that, while one of these parts, that which represented the more material side of the science in question, took on an independent development, the other part, on the other hand, disappeared entirely. This is so true that we no longer know what ancient astrology was, and that those who have tried to reconstitute it have only come up with genuine counterfeits, either by trying to make it the equivalent of a modern experimental science, with the intervention of statistics and the calculation of probabilities, This is the result of a point of view that could in no way be that of antiquity or the Middle Ages, or of an exclusive attempt to restore a "divinatory art" that was little more than a deviation from astrology on its way to extinction, and in which one could at best see a very inferior application, not worthy of much consideration, as can still be seen in Eastern civilizations.

The case of chemistry is perhaps even clearer and more characteristic, and modern ignorance of alchemy is at least as great as that of astrology. True alchemy was essentially a science of the cosmological order, and at the same time applicable to the human order too, by virtue of the analogy of the "macrocosm" and the "microcosm"; moreover, it was expressly constituted with a view to enabling a transposition into the purely spiritual realm, which conferred on its teachings a symbolic value and a superior significance, and made it one of the most complete types of "traditional science". What gave rise to modern chemistry was not alchemy, with which it bears no relation whatsoever; it was a deformation, a deviation in the strictest sense of the word, a deviation which, perhaps as early as the Middle Ages, was caused by the incomprehension of some who, unable to grasp the true meaning of the symbols, took everything lite-rally and, believing that it was all about material operations, embarked on more or less haphazard experimentation. It was these, whom the alchemists ironically described as "blowers" and "charcoal burners", who were the real fore-runners of today's chemists; and so it is that modern science is built on the debris of the ancient sciences, with the mate-rials rejected by the latter and abandoned to the ignorant and "profane". Let us add that the so-called renovators of alchemy, of whom there are a few among our contempora-ries, for their part only prolong this same deviation, and that their research is as far removed from traditional alchemy as that of the astrologers to whom we referred earlier is from ancient astrology; and this is why we have the right to assert that the "traditional sciences" of the West are truly lost to the modern.

We'll confine ourselves to these few examples; it would be easy, however, to give others, taken from somewhat dif-ferent orders, and showing the same degeneration everywhere. We could thus show that psychology as we un-derstand it today, i.e. the study of mental phenomena as such, is a natural product of Anglo-Saxon empiricism and the spi-rit of the eighteenth century, and that the point of view to which it corresponds was so negligible for the ancients that, even if they sometimes incidentally considered it, they would never have thought of making it a special science; For them, anything of value in it was transformed and assimi-lated into higher points of view. In a completely different field, we could also show that modern mathematics repre-sents, so to speak, only the bark of Pythagorean mathema-tics, its purely "exoteric" side; the ancient idea of numbers has even become absolutely unintelligible to modern people, because here too, the higher part of the science, that which gave it, along with its traditional character, a properly intellectual value, has completely disappeared; and this case is quite comparable to that of astrology. But we can't go through all the sciences one after the other, which would be rather tedious; we think we've said enough to make clear the nature of the change to which the modern sciences owe their origin, and which is the very opposite of "progress", which is a veritable regression of intelligence; and we shall now return to general considerations on the respective roles of the "traditional sciences" and the modern sciences, on the profound difference that exists between the true destination of the one and the other.

Any science, according to the traditional conception, is less interesting in itself than in that it is as an extension or secondary branch of doctrine, the essential part of which is, as we have said, pure metaphysics[4]. Indeed, while any science is certainly legitimate, as long as it occupies only the place that is really appropriate to its own nature, it is nevertheless easy to understand that, for anyone who possesses knowledge of a higher order, inferior knowledge necessarily loses much of its interest, and even retains it only as a function, so to speak, that is, insofar as, on the one hand, they reflect the latter in this or that contingent domain, and, on the other, they are likely to lead to this same principial knowledge, which, in the case we are considering, can never be lost sight of or sacrificed to more or less accidental considerations. These are the two complementary roles of the "traditional sciences": on the one hand, as applications of doctrine, they enable us to link together all orders of reality, to integrate them into the unity of a total synthesis; on the other hand, they are, for some at least, and in accordance with their aptitudes, a preparation for higher knowledge, a kind of pathway to the latter, and, in their hierarchical distribution according to the degrees of existence to which they relate, they then constitute like so many rungs by means of which it is possible to rise to pure intellectuality[5]. It is all too clear that modern science can fulfill neither of these two roles to any degree, which is why it is and can only be "profane science", whereas "traditional science", by virtue of its connection to metaphysical principles, is effectively incorporated into "sacred science".

The coexistence of these two roles does not imply any contradiction or vicious circle, contrary to what those who take a superficial view of things might think. We could say that there are two points of view here, one descending and the other ascending, the first corresponding to a development of knowledge starting from principles and going on to applications further and further away from them, and the second to a gradual acquisition of this same knowledge by proceeding from the inferior to the superior, or, if we prefer, from the exterior to the interior. The question, then, is not whether the sciences should be constituted from the bottom up or from the top down, or whether, in order to be possible, they should take as their starting point knowledge of principles or, on the contrary, knowledge of the sensible world ; this question, which may arise from the point of view of "profane" philosophy, and which seems to have been posed in this field, more or less explicitly, by Greek antiquity, this question, we say, does not exist for "sacred science", which can only start from universal principles; And what makes it irrelevant here is the primary role of intellectual intuition, which is the most immediate of all forms of knowledge, as well as the highest, and absolutely independent of the exercise of any sensible or even rational faculty. The sciences can only be validly constituted as "sacred sciences" by those who, first and foremost, fully possess principial knowledge, and who are therefore uniquely qualified to carry out, in accordance with the most rigorous traditional orthodoxy, all the adaptations required by the circumstances of time and place. However, when the sciences are constituted in this way, their teaching can follow a reverse order: they are, in a way, like "illustrations" of pure doctrine, which can make it more easily accessible to certain minds; and, by the very fact that they concern the world of multiplicity, the almost indefinite diversity of their points of view can suit the no less great diversity of the individual aptitudes of these minds, whose horizon is still limited to this same world of multiplicity; the possible paths to knowledge can be extremely different in the lowest degree, and they then go on unifying more and more as we reach higher stages. It's not that any of these preparatory stages are absolutely necessary, since they are merely contingent means out of all proportion to the goal to be achieved; it may even be that some, among those in whom the contemplative tendency dominates, rise to true intellectual intuition all at once and without the aid of such means[6]; but this is a rather exceptional case, and, more usually, there is what we might call a necessity of convenience in proceeding in the upward direction. We can also use the traditional image of the "cosmic wheel" to make this point: the circumference really only exists through the center; but beings on the circumference must necessarily start from the circumference, or more precisely from the point on the circumference where they are located, and follow the radius to the center. Moreover, by virtue of the correspondence that exists between all orders of reality, the truths of a lower order can be considered as a symbol of those of higher orders, and, consequently, serve as a "support" for arriving analogically at knowledge of the latter[7] ; this is what confers on all science a higher or "anagogical" meaning, deeper than that which it possesses on its own, and what can give it the character of a true "sacred science".

All sciences, we say, can assume this character, whatever their object, on the sole condition of being constituted and envisaged according to the traditional spirit; in this, we need only take into account the degrees of importance of these sciences, according to the hierarchical rank of the various realities to which they relate; but, to one degree or another, their character and function are essentially the same in the traditional conception. What is true here of all science is also true of all art, insofar as the latter can have a properly symbolic value that makes it suitable for providing "supports" for meditation, and also insofar as its rules are, like the laws whose knowledge is the object of the sciences, reflections and applications of fundamental principles; and so there are, in every normal civilization, "traditional arts", which are no less unknown to modern Westerners than "traditional sciences"[8]. The truth is that there is no such thing as a "profane realm", which is in some way opposed to the "sacred realm"; there is only a "profane point of view", which is properly nothing other than the point of view of ignorance[9]. That's why "profane science", as we've already said elsewhere, can rightly be regarded as "ignorant knowledge": knowledge of an inferior order, holding itself entirely at the level of the lowest reality, and ignorant of all that goes beyond it, ignorant of any end higher than itself, as well as of any principle that could assure it a legitimate place, however humble, among the various orders of integral knowledge;

irremediably enclosed in the relative and limited domain in which it has sought to proclaim itself independent, having thus cut itself off from all communication with transcendent truth and supreme knowledge, it is nothing more than a vain and illusory science, which, in truth, comes from nothing and leads to nothing.

This presentation will help us to understand what the modern world lacks in the way of science, and how the very science of which it is so proud represents nothing more than a deviation and a waste product from true science, which, for us, is entirely identified with what we have called "sacred science" or "traditional science". Modern science, proceeding from an arbitrary limitation of knowledge to a certain particular order, which is the most inferior of all, that of material or sensible reality, has lost, because of this limitation and the consequences it immediately entails, all intellectual value, at least if we give intellectuality the fullness of its true meaning, if we refuse to share the "rationalist" error, i.e. to equate pure intelligence with reason, or, what amounts to the same thing, to deny intellectual intuition. What lies at the root of this error, as of a large proportion of other modern errors, what lies at the root of the whole deviation of science as we have just explained it, is what we can call "individualism", which is one and the same with the anti-traditional spirit itself, and whose multiple manifestations, in all fields, constitute one of the most important factors in the disorder of our times; It is this "individualism" that we must now examine more closely.

1 - It may be noted that something similar has happened in the social order, where moderns have claimed to separate the temporal from the spiritual; this is not to deny that there are two distinct things here, since they do indeed relate to different domains, as in the case of metaphysics and the sciences; but, through an error inherent in the analytical mind, we forget that distinction does not mean separation; in this way, temporal power loses its legitimacy, and the same could be said, in the intellectual order, of the sciences.

2 - The same observation applies, from a religious point of view, to a certain "apologetics" which claims to be in harmony with the results of modern science, a perfectly illusory task which must always be redone, and which presents the serious danger of appearing to tie religion in with changing and ephemeral conceptions, from which it must remain totally independent.

3 - It would be easy to give examples here; we'll just mention, as one of the most striking, the difference in character of conceptions concerning the ether in Hindu cosmology and modern physics.

4 - This is expressed, for example, by a term like *upavêda*, applied in India to certain "traditional sciences", and indicating their subordination to the *Vêda*, i.e. to sacred knowledge par excellence.

5 - In our study The *Esotericism of Dante,* we indicated the symbolism of the ladder whose rungs, according to various traditions, correspond to certain sciences as well as states of being, which necessarily implies that these sciences, instead of being considered in a wholly "profane" manner as in modern times, gave rise to a transposition conferring on them a truly "initiatory" scope.

6 - This is why, according to Hindu doctrine, Brahmins sould keep their minds constantly turned towars suprem knowledge, whereas Kshatriyas should rather apply themselves to study of the successive stages by which this gradually to be reached.

7 - This is the role played, for example, by the astronomical symbolism so frequently employed in the various traditional doctrines; and what we say here may give a glimpse of the true nature of a science such as ancient astrology.

8 - The art of medieval builders can be mentioned as a particularly remarkable example of these "traditional arts", the practice of which implied a real knowledge of the corresponding sciences.

9 - To convince ourselves of this, we need only observe facts such as the following: one of the most "sacred" sciences, cosmogony, which has its place as such in all the inspired Books, including the Hebrew Bible, has become, for moderns, the object of the most purely "profane" hypotheses; the field of science is indeed the same in both cases, but the point of view is totally different.

CHAPTER V

INDIVIDUALISM

What we mean by "individualism" is the negation of any principle higher than individuality, and consequently the reduction of civilization in all fields to purely human elements; it is therefore basically the same thing as what was referred to during the Renaissance as "humanism", as we said earlier, and it is also what properly characterizes what we just called the "profane point of view". All this, in short, is one and the same thing under different names; and we've already said that this "profane" spirit merges with the anti-traditional spirit, in which all specifically modern tendencies are summed up. Of course, it's not that this spirit is entirely new; in other eras, it has already had more or less accentuated manifestations, but always limited and aberrant, and never extended to the whole of a civilization as it has done in the West in recent centuries. What has never been seen before is a civilization built entirely on something purely negative, on what we might call an absence of principle; this is precisely what gives the modern world its abnormal character, what makes it a kind of monstrosity, explicable only if we consider it as corresponding to the end of a cyclical period, as we explained earlier. It is therefore individualism, as we have just defined it, that is the determining cause of the West's present decline, in that it is in some way the driving force behind the exclusive development of humanity's most inferior possibilities, those whose expansion does not require the intervention of any supra-human element, and which can only fully unfold in the absence of such an element, because they are the very opposite of all spirituality and all true intellectuality.

First of all, individualism implies the negation of intellectual intuition, insofar as it is essentially a supra-individual faculty, and of the order of knowledge that is the proper domain of this intuition, i.e. metaphysics understood in its true sense. This is why everything that modern philosophers designate under this same name of metaphysics, when they admit something they call so, has absolutely nothing in common with true metaphysics: they are nothing but rational constructions or imaginative hypotheses, and therefore entirely individual conceptions, most of which, moreover, simply relate to the "physical" domain, i.e. to nature. Even if there is a question in there that could be effectively linked to the metaphysical order, the way it is envisaged and dealt with still reduces it to nothing more than "pseudo-metaphysics ", and makes any real, valid solution impossible; It even seems that, for philosophers, it's a question of posing "problems", however artificial and illusory, rather than solving them, which is one of the aspects of the disordered need for research for its own sake, i.e. of the most futile agitation in the mental order, as well as in the bodily order. For these same philosophers, it's also a question of attaching their name to a "system", i.e., to a strictly limited and delimited set of theories, that is their own, that is nothing other than their own work; hence the desire to be original at all costs, even if truth must be sacrificed to this originality: better, for a philosopher's fame, to invent a new error than to repeat a truth that has already been expressed by others. This form of individualism, to which we owe so many mutually contradictory "systems", when they are not contradictory in themselves, is just as common among modern scientists and artists; but it is perhaps among philosophers that we can see most clearly the intellectual anarchy that is its inevitable consequence.

In a traditional civilization, it is almost inconceivable that a man should claim ownership of an idea, and in any case, if he does so, he thereby takes away all credit and authority from himself, for he reduces it to being no more than a kind of fantasy with no real significance: if an idea is true, it belongs equally to all those who are capable of understanding it; if it is false, there is no glory in having invented it. A true idea cannot be "new", because truth is not a product of the human mind, it exists independently of us, and we only have to know it; outside this knowledge, there can only be error; but, really, do modern people care about truth, and do they even know what it is anymore? Here, too, words have lost their meaning, since some, like the contemporary "pragmatists", go so far as to misleadingly give the name "truth" to what is quite simply practical utility, i.e. to something that is entirely foreign to the intellectual order; this is, as the logical outcome of the modern deviation, the very negation of truth, as well as of the intelligence of which it is the proper object. But let's not anticipate any further, and on this point, let's just point out again that the kind of individualism we've just been talking about is the source of illusions about the role of "great men" or so-called "great men"; "genius", understood in the "profane" sense, is very little in reality, and can in no way make up for the lack of true knowledge.

While we're on the subject of philosophy, let's not go into detail about some of the consequences of individualism in this field: first and foremost, by negating intellectual intuition, we put reason above all else, making this purely human and relative faculty the superior part of the intelligence, or even reducing the latter to it altogether; this is what constitutes "rationalism", whose true founder was Descartes. This limitation of the intellect was only the first step, however; reason itself was soon to be increasingly reduced to a primarily practical role, as applications took precedence over sciences that might still have a certain speculative character; and Descartes himself was already much more concerned with these practical applications than with pure science. But that's not all: individualism inevitably leads to "naturalism", since everything beyond nature is, by the same token, beyond the reach of the individual as such; "naturalism" or the negation of metaphysics are, in fact, one and the same thing, and once intellectual intuition has been disregarded, metaphysics is no longer possible; But while some persist in building a "pseudo-metaphysics" of some kind, others more frankly recognize this impossibility; hence "relativism" in all its forms, whether Kant's "criticism" or Auguste Comte's "positivism"; and, reason being itself all relative and only validly applicable to an equally relative domain, it is quite true that "relativism" is the only logical outcome of "rationalism". Rationalism was bound to destroy itself in the process: "Nature" and "becoming", as we noted above, are in fact synonymous; a "naturalism" consistent with itself can therefore only be one of those "philosophies of becoming" we've already mentioned, the specifically modern type of which is "evolutionism"; but it is precisely this that was ultimately to turn against "rationalism", by reproaching reason with being unable to apply itself adequately to what is only change and pure multiplicity, nor to enclose in its concepts the indefinite complexity of sensible things. This is the position taken by Bergsonian intuitionism, a form of "evolutionism" which, of course, is no less individualistic and anti-metaphysical than "rationalism", and which, while criticizing the latter, falls even lower by appealing to a properly infra-rational faculty, to a rather ill-defined sensitive intuition, more or less mixed with imagination, instinct and feeling. Significantly, here there is no longer even any question of "truth", but only of "reality", reduced exclusively to the sensible order, and conceived as something essentially shifting and unstable; intelligence, with such theories, is truly reduced to its lowest part, and reason itself is only admitted insofar as it applies itself to shaping matter for industrial uses. After that, there was only one step left to take: the total negation of intelligence and knowledge, the substitution of "utility" for "truth"; this was "pragmatism", to which we alluded earlier; and here, we are no longer even in the purely human as with "rationalism", we are truly in the infrahuman, with the appeal to the "subconscious" that marks the complete reversal of all normal hierarchy. As long as superior knowledge existed, nothing of the kind could happen, for philosophy was at least bound to respect what it did not know, and could not deny it. But when this superior knowledge disappeared, its negation, which corresponded to the state of affairs, was soon erected as a theory, and it is from this that all modern philosophy proceeds.

But that's enough about philosophy, to which we shouldn't attribute excessive importance, whatever place it seems to hold in the modern world; from our point of view, it is above all interesting in that it expresses, in as clearly defined a form as possible, the tendencies of this or that moment, rather than actually creating them; and, if we can say that it directs them to a certain point, it is only secondarily and after the fact. Thus, it is certain that all modern philosophy has its origins in Descartes; but the influence he exerted on his own era first, and then on those that followed, and which was not limited to philosophers alone, would not have been possible if his conceptions had not corresponded to pre-existing tendencies, which were in short those of the generality of his contemporaries; The modern mind found itself in Cartesianism and, through it, became more clearly aware of itself than it had been until then. Moreover, in any field, a movement as apparent as Cartesianism was in philosophical terms is always a result rather than a true point of departure; it is not something spontaneous, it is the product of a whole latent and diffuse work; If a man like Descartes is particularly representative of the modern deviation, if he can be said to embody it to a certain extent from a certain point of view, he is nevertheless not the only one or the one primarily responsible for it, and we would have to go back much further to find the roots of this deviation. In the same way, the Renaissance and Reformation, which are most often regarded as the first great manifestations of the modern spirit, completed the break with tradition much more than they provoked it; for us, the beginning of this break dates from the fourteenth century, and it is here, and not one or two centuries later, that modern times really begin.

It is this break with tradition that we must insist on, since it is from this break that the modern world was born, and all its characteristics can be summed up in a single one: opposition to the traditional spirit; and the negation of tradition is individualism. This, moreover, is in perfect accord with what has gone before, since, as we have explained, it is intellectual intuition and pure metaphysical doctrine that are at the root of all traditional civilization; as soon as one denies the principle, one also denies all its consequences, at least implicitly, and thus the whole of what truly deserves the name of tradition is thereby destroyed. We've already seen what has happened in this respect in the sciences, so we won't come back to it, and will consider another side of the question, where the manifestations of the anti-traditional spirit are perhaps even more immediately visible, because here we're dealing with changes that have directly affected the Western mass itself. Indeed, the "traditional sciences" of the Middle Ages were reserved for a more or less restricted elite, and some of them were even the exclusive prerogative of very closed schools, constituting "esotericism" in the strictest sense of the word; but, on the other hand, there was also, within tradition, something that was common to all indiscriminately, and it's this outer part that we want to talk about now. Western tradition was then, outwardly, a tradition of specifically religious form, represented by Catholicism; so it's in the religious realm that we're going to have to consider the revolt against the traditional spirit, a revolt which, when it took on a definite form, was called Protestantism; and it's easy to realize that this is indeed a manifestation of individualism, so much so that we could say it's nothing other than individualism itself considered in its application to religion. Protestantism, like the modern world, is all about negation, the negation of principles that is the very essence of individualism; and here again we see one of the most striking examples of the state of anarchy and dissolution that is its consequence.

Individualism necessarily means refusing to accept an authority superior to the individual, as well as a faculty of knowledge superior to individual reason; the two things are inseparable from each other. Consequently, the modern mind had to reject all spiritual authority in the true sense of the word, which has its source in the supra-human order, and all traditional organization, which is essentially based on such authority, whatever form it takes - a form which naturally differs according to civilization. This is indeed what happened: in place of the authority of the organization qualified to legitimately interpret the religious tradition of the West, Protestantism claimed to substitute what it called "free examination", i.e. interpretation left to the arbitrariness of each individual, even the ignorant and incompetent, and based solely on the exercise of human reason. In the religious sphere, therefore, it was the analogue of what "rationalism" was to be in philosophy; it opened the door to all manner of discussion, divergence and deviation; and the result was what it was supposed to be: dispersion into an ever-growing multitude of sects, each of which represented no more than the particular opinion of a few individuals. Since it was impossible to agree on doctrine in such conditions, doctrine soon took a back seat, and it was the secondary side of religion, by which we mean morality, that came to the fore: hence the degeneration into "moralism" that is so noticeable in Protestantism today. The doctrinal dissolution, the disappearance of the intellectual elements of religion, led to this inevitable consequence: from "rationalism", we had to fall to "sentimentalism", and it's in the Anglo-Saxon countries that we can find the most striking examples . What we're dealing with here is no longer religion, even if it's lessened and distorted, but simply "religiosity", i.e. vague sentimental aspirations unjustified by any real knowledge; and to this last stage correspond such theories as William James's "religious experience", which goes so far as to see the "subconscious" as man's means of entering into communication with the divine. Here, the last products of religious decay merge with those of philosophical decay: religious experience" is incorporated into "pragmatism", in the name of which the idea of a limited God is advocated as more "advantageous" than that of the infinite God, because we can have feelings for him comparable to those we have for a superior man; and, at the same time, by appealing to the "subconscious", we come to join spiritualism and all the "pseudo-religions" characteristic of our time, which we have studied in other works. On the other hand, Protestant morality, increasingly eliminating any doctrinal basis, ends up degenerating into what is known as "profane morality", which counts among its supporters representatives of all varieties of "liberal Protestantism", as well as declared opponents of any religious idea; basically, in both, the same tendencies predominate, the only difference being that not all go as far in the logical development of everything involved.

Indeed, since religion is properly a form of tradition, the anti-traditional spirit can only be anti-religious; it begins by denaturing religion, and, when it can, ends by suppressing it entirely. Protestantism is illogical in that, while it strives to "humanize" religion, it nonetheless allows a supra-human element to remain, at least in theory, which is revelation; it does not dare push negation to the limit, but, by handing over this revelation to all the discussions that are the consequence of purely human interpretations, it reduces it in fact to being soon nothing ; And when we see people who, while persisting in calling themselves "Christians", no longer even admit the divinity of Christ, it's safe to assume that these people, perhaps without realizing it, are much closer to complete denial than to true Christianity. Such contradictions, moreover, should come as no great surprise, for they are, in every field, one of the symptoms of our age of disorder and confusion, just as the incessant division of Protestantism is only one of the many manifestations of that dispersion in multiplicity which, as we have said, is to be found everywhere in modern life and science. On the other hand, it is natural that Protestantism, with the spirit of negation that animates it, should have given birth to that dissolving "critique" which, in the hands of the so-called "historians of religions", has become a weapon of combat against all religion, and that thus, while claiming to recognize no other authority than that of the Sacred Books, it has contributed to a large extent to the destruction of this same authority, i.e. of the minimum of tradition that it still preserved; the revolt against the traditional spirit, once begun, could not stop halfway.

An objection could be raised here: wouldn't it have been possible for Protestantism, while separating itself from the Catholic organization, to keep the traditional doctrine contained in the Sacred Books, even though it admitted them? It's the introduction of "free examination" that absolutely opposes such a hypothesis, since it allows for all sorts of individual fantasies; moreover, the preservation of doctrine presupposes an organized traditional teaching, through which orthodox interpretation is maintained, and in fact, this teaching, in the Western world, was identified with Catholicism. Undoubtedly, in other civilizations, there may be organizations of very different forms to fulfil the corresponding function; but it's Western civilization, with its particular conditions, that we're talking about here. It cannot therefore be argued that, for example, no institution comparable to the Papacy exists in India; The case is quite different, firstly because we are not dealing with a tradition of religious form in the Western sense of the word, so the means by which it is preserved and transmitted cannot be the same, and secondly because, the Hindu mind being quite different from the European mind, tradition can have by itself, in the first case, a power that it could not have in the second without the support of an organization much more strictly defined in its external constitution. We have already said that Western tradition, from Christianity onwards, must necessarily be clothed in a religious form; it would take too long to explain here all the reasons for this, which cannot be fully understood without recourse to some rather complex considerations; but it is a state of affairs which we cannot refuse to take into account[1], and, consequently, we must also admit all the consequences which result from it with regard to the organization appropriate to such a traditional form.

On the other hand, it is quite certain, as we also pointed out above, that it is in Catholicism alone that what remains of the traditional spirit in the West has been preserved. Does this mean that, here at least, we can speak of a complete preservation of tradition, sheltered from any attack by the modern spirit? Unfortunately, this does not seem to be the case; or, to put it more accurately, if the deposit of tradition has remained intact, which is already a great deal, it is rather doubtful whether its deeper meaning is still effectively understood, even by a small elite, whose existence would undoubtedly be manifested by an action or rather by an influence that, in fact, we see nowhere. It's more likely, then, that we're dealing with what we'd like to call a latent state of conservation, which will always enable those who are capable of it to rediscover the meaning of tradition, even if this meaning is not currently conscious for anyone; and there are also, moreover, scattered here and there in the Western world, outside the religious domain, many signs or symbols which come from ancient traditional doctrines, and which are preserved without being understood. In such cases, contact with the fully living traditional spirit is necessary to awaken what is thus plunged into a kind of sleep, to restore lost understanding; and, let us repeat once again, it is in this respect above all that the West will need the help of the East if it is to return to an awareness of its own tradition.

Here, therefore, the influence of the modern mind is necessarily limited to preventing, for a more or less long period, certain things from being effectively understood. On the other hand, if, in speaking of the present state of Catholicism, we were to understand the way in which it is viewed by the vast majority of its adherents, we would be obliged to note a more positive action of the modern spirit, if this expression can be used for something which, in reality, is essentially negative. What we have in mind here is not only movements that are quite clearly defined, such as the one to which the name "modernism" has been given, and which was nothing more than an attempt, fortunately thwarted, to infiltrate the Protestant spirit into the Catholic Church itself; it is above all a much more general state of mind, more diffuse and more difficult to grasp, and therefore even more dangerous, all the more so because it is often completely unconscious in those who are affected by it: You can even call yourself a "traditionalist" without having the slightest notion of the true traditional spirit, and this too is one of the symptoms of the mental disorder of our times. The state of mind to which we allude is, first and foremost, that which consists, so to speak, in "minimizing" religion, in making it something that is set apart, to which we are content to assign a place that is well-defined and as narrow as possible, something that has no real influence on the rest of existence, that is isolated from it by a kind of watertight partition; Are there many Catholics today who, in everyday life, think and act in ways that are markedly different from those of their more "areligious" contemporaries? There is also almost complete ignorance of doctrinal matters, and even indifference to anything related to them; religion, for many, is simply a matter of "practice", of habit, not to say routine, and we carefully refrain from trying to understand anything about it, we even come to think that it's useless to understand, or perhaps that there's nothing to understand; besides, if we really understood religion, could we give it such a mediocre place among our preoccupations? Doctrine is thus, in fact, forgotten or reduced to almost nothing, which is singularly close to the Protestant conception, because it is an effect of the same modern tendencies, opposed to all intellectuality; and what is most deplorable is that the teaching that is generally given, instead of reacting against this state of mind, on the contrary favors it by adapting to it only too well: religion is now no more than "moralism", or at least no one seems to want to see what it really is, which is something quite different. If, however, we still sometimes talk about doctrine, it is all too often only to belittle it by arguing with opponents on their own "profane" terrain, which inevitably leads to making the most unjustified concessions to them; This is how, for example, we feel obliged to take into account, to a greater or lesser extent, the so-called results of modern "criticism", when nothing would be easier, from a different point of view, than to demonstrate their utter futility. Under these conditions, what can remain of the true traditional spirit?

This digression, to which we have been led by the examination of the manifestations of individualism in the religious sphere, does not seem to us to be in vain, for it shows that the evil, in this respect, is even more serious and more widespread than might be thought at first sight; and, on the other hand, it hardly distances us from the question we were considering, and to which our last remark is even directly related, for it is again individualism that introduces everywhere the spirit of discussion. It is very difficult to make our contemporaries understand that there are things which, by their very nature, cannot be discussed; modern man, instead of seeking to elevate himself to the truth, pretends to bring it down to his level; and this is undoubtedly why there are so many who, when we speak to them of "traditional sciences" or even of pure metaphysics, imagine that it is only a question of "profane science" and "philosophy". In the realm of individual opinions, we can always argue, because we don't go beyond the rational order, and because, appealing to no higher principle, we can easily find more or less valid arguments to support the "for" and the "against"; we can even, in many cases, push the discussion on indefinitely without reaching any solution, and this is how almost all modern philosophy is made up of equivocations and ill-posed questions. Far from clarifying questions as is usually supposed, discussion more often than not does little more than displace them, if not obscure them further; and the most usual result is that everyone, in striving to convince his opponent, becomes more attached than ever to his own opinion, and locks himself into it even more exclusively than before. At the end of the day, it's not about getting to the truth, it's about being right in spite of everything, or at least persuading yourself, if you can't persuade others - which is all the more regrettable given that the need to "proselytize" is still one of the most characteristic elements of the Western mindset. Sometimes, individualism, in the most ordinary and basest sense of the word, manifests itself in an even more apparent way: for example, don't we always see people who want to judge a man's work on the basis of what they know about his private life, as if there could be any connection between these two things ? The same tendency, combined with a mania for detail, is also behind the interest we take in the slightest particularities of the lives of "great men", and the illusion we have of explaining everything they have done by a kind of "psycho-physiological" analysis; all this is very significant for those who want to understand what contemporary mentality really is.

But let's go back for a moment to the introduction of discussion habits in areas where they have no business, and let's say this clearly: the "apologetic" attitude is, in itself, an extremely weak attitude, because it is purely "defensive", in the legal sense of the word ; it's not for nothing that it's designated by a term derived from "apology", whose proper meaning is a lawyer's plea, and which, in a language such as English, has gone so far as to commonly take on the meaning of "apology"; the overriding importance accorded to "apologetics" is therefore the unmistakable mark of a retreat in the religious spirit. This weakness is further accentuated when "apologetics" degenerates, as we said earlier, into discussions that are all "profane" in method and point of view, where religion is placed on the same level as the most contingent and hypothetical philosophical and scientific, or pseudo-scientific, theories, and where, in order to appear "conciliatory", one goes so far as to admit to a certain extent conceptions that have been invented only to ruin all religion ; those who act in this way are themselves proof that they are blissfully unaware of the true character of the doctrine of which they believe themselves to be the more or less authorized representatives. Those who are qualified to speak in the name of a traditional doctrine have no business arguing with "laymen" or engaging in "polemics"; they have only to set out the doctrine as it is, for those who can understand it, and, at the same time, to denounce error wherever it is found, to make it appear as such by projecting the light of true knowledge onto it; Their role is not to engage in a battle and compromise doctrine, but to make the judgement they are entitled to make if they actually possess the principles that should infallibly inspire them... The domain of struggle is that of action, i.e. the individual and temporal domain; the "immovable motor" produces and directs movement without being drawn into it; knowledge enlightens action without participating in its vicissitudes; the spiritual guides the temporal without interfering with it; and so everything remains in its proper order, in its proper place in the universal hierarchy; but, in the modern world, where can we still find the notion of a true hierarchy? Nothing and no-one is in the place they should normally be; men no longer recognize any effective authority in the spiritual order, any legitimate power in the temporal order; the "profane" take the liberty of discussing sacred things, disputing their character and even their very existence; It's the inferior judging the superior, ignorance imposing limits on wisdom, error taking precedence over truth, the human replacing the divine, earth prevailing over heaven, the individual making himself the measure of all things and claiming to dictate to the universe laws drawn entirely from his own relative and fallible reason. "Woe to you, blind guides", it says in the Gospel; today, indeed, we see everywhere only blind people leading other blind people, and who, if they are not stopped in time, will fatally lead them to the abyss where they will perish with them.

1 - According to the Gospel, this state of affairs must be maintained until the "consummation of the age", i.e. until the end of the current cycle.

CHAPTER VI

THE SOCIAL CHAOS

In this study, we do not intend to focus specifically on the social point of view, which interests us only very indirectly, because it represents only a rather remote application of fundamental principles, and consequently it is not in this field that a recovery of the modern world could, in any case, begin. Indeed, if such a turnaround were to be undertaken in reverse, i.e. starting from consequences instead of principles, it would necessarily lack any serious basis and would be completely illusory; nothing stable could ever result, and everything would have to be restarted incessantly, because we would have neglected to agree first and foremost on the essential truths. This is why it is not possible for us to accord political contingencies, even in the broadest sense of the word, any value other than that of mere external signs of the mentality of an age; but, in this very respect, neither can we pass entirely over in silence the manifestations of modern disorder in the social sphere proper.

As we pointed out earlier, in the present state of the Western world, no one is in the place that normally befits him by virtue of his own nature; this is what we mean when we say that castes no longer exist, for caste, understood in its true traditional sense, is nothing other than individual nature itself, with all the special aptitudes it entails and which predispose each man to the accomplishment of this or that specific function. As soon as access to any function is no longer subject to any legitimate rule, the inevitable result is that everyone will find themselves doing anything, and often what they are least qualified to do; the role he will play in society will be determined, not by chance, which does not exist in reality[1], but by what can give the illusion of chance, i.e., by the tangle of all sorts of accidental circumstances; what will intervene least will be precisely the only factor that should count in such a case, i.e., the differences in nature that exist between men. The cause of all this disorder is the negation of these differences themselves, leading to the negation of all social hierarchy; and this negation, at first perhaps scarcely conscious and more practical than theoretical, for the confusion of castes preceded their complete abolition, or, in other words, we misunderstood the nature of individuals before coming to take no account of it, this negation, we say, was then erected by moderns as a pseudo-principle under the name of "equality". It would be all too easy to show that equality cannot exist anywhere, for the simple reason that there can be no two beings who are both truly distinct and entirely similar to each other in every respect ; and it would be no less easy to point out all the absurd consequences that flow from this chimerical idea, in the name of which we pretend to impose complete uniformity everywhere, for example by distributing identical teaching to everyone, as if everyone were equally capable of understanding the same things, and as if, to make them understand, the same methods were suitable for everyone indiscriminately. We might also ask whether it's not more a question of "learning" than of truly "understanding", i.e. whether memory has not been substituted for intelligence in the all-verbal, "bookish" conception of today's education, where the aim is only to accumulate rudimentary, heterogeneous notions, and where quality is entirely sacrificed to quantity, as happens everywhere in the modern world for reasons we'll explain more fully later: it's always dispersion in multiplicity. But this is not the place to dwell on the subject, and so as not to stray from the framework we have drawn up for ourselves, we must content ourselves with pointing out in passing this special consequence of "egalitarian" theories, as one of those elements of disorder that are too numerous today for us to even pretend to enumerate them without omitting any.

Naturally, when we find ourselves in the presence of an idea like "equality", or "progress", or the other "profane dogmas" that almost all our contemporaries blindly accept, and most of which began to be clearly formulated during the eighteenth century, we can't admit that such ideas arose spontaneously. In short, they are genuine "suggestions", in the strictest sense of the word , which could only produce their effect in an environment already prepared to receive them; they didn't create from scratch the state of mind that characterizes the modern era, but they largely contributed to nurturing and developing it to a point it would probably not have reached without them. This is why they are so carefully nurtured by all those who have an interest in maintaining disorder, if not in aggravating it, and why, in an age when everything is supposed to be open to discussion, they are the only things we never allow ourselves to discuss. It is difficult, moreover, to determine exactly how sincere are those who propagate such ideas, to know to what extent certain men come to be taken in by their own lies, and to suggest themselves by suggesting others; and even, in propaganda of this kind, those who play the role of dupes are often the best instruments, because they bring to it a conviction that others would find difficult to simulate, and which is easily contagious; but, behind all this, and at least at the outset, there must be a much more conscious action, a direction that can only come from men who know perfectly well where they stand on the ideas they are thus putting into circulation. We have spoken of "ideas", but this word can only be applied very loosely here, for it is quite obvious that these are not pure ideas, nor even anything remotely related to the intellectual order; they are, if you like, false ideas, but it would be better to call them "pseudo-ideas", intended mainly to provoke sentimental reactions, which is indeed the most effective and easy way of acting on the masses. In this respect, the word is of greater importance than the notion it is supposed to represent, and most modern "idols" are really just words, for here we have that peculiar phenomenon known as "verbalism", where the sound of words is enough to give the illusion of thought; The influence that orators exert on crowds is particularly characteristic in this respect, and we don't need to study it very closely to realize that it is indeed a process of suggestion quite comparable to those of hypnotists.

But, without dwelling further on these considerations, let's return to the consequences of negating any real hierarchy, and note that, in the present state of affairs, not only does a man fulfill his proper function only exceptionally and as if by accident, whereas the opposite should normally be the exception, but it also happens that the same man is called upon to successively exercise quite different functions, as if he could change aptitudes at will. This may seem paradoxical in an age of excessive "specialization", but it is indeed the case, especially in the political arena. Although the competence of "specialists" is often illusory, and in any case limited to a very narrow field, belief in this competence is nevertheless a fact, and we may wonder why this belief no longer plays any role when it comes to the careers of politicians, where complete incompetence is rarely an obstacle. Yet, on reflection, it's easy to see that there's nothing to be surprised about, and that it's really just a very natural result of the "democratic" conception, according to which power comes from below and is essentially based on the majority, which necessarily excludes any real competence, because competence is always at least a relative superiority and can only be the prerogative of a minority.

It is almost superfluous, given the point of view we are taking, to point out that these observations will be formulated outside of all party issues and political quarrels, in which we do not intend to get involved either directly or remotely. We are looking at these things in an absolutely disinterested way, as we could do for any other object of study, and seeking only to realize as clearly as possible what lies at the heart of it all, which is, incidentally, the necessary and sufficient condition for dispelling any illusions our contemporaries may have about the subject. Here, too, we are dealing with "suggestion", as we said earlier about ideas that are somewhat different, but nonetheless related; and, as soon as we know that it's only a suggestion, as soon as we understand how it works, it can no longer be exercised; against things of this kind, a somewhat thorough and purely "objective" examination, as we say today in the special jargon borrowed from the German philosophers, is far more effective than all the sentimental declamations and all the party polemics, which prove nothing and are merely the expression of individual preferences.

The most decisive argument against "democracy" can be summed up in a few words: the superior cannot emanate from the inferior, because "more" cannot emanate from "less"; this is an absolute mathematical rigor, against which nothing can prevail. It's important to note that it's precisely the same argument that, applied in another order, also applies against "materialism"; there's nothing fortuitous about this concordance, and the two things are much more closely intertwined than might at first appear. True power can only come from above, and that's why, let us say in passing, it can only be legitimized by the sanction of something higher than the social order, i.e., a spiritual authority; otherwise, it is no more than a counterfeit of power, a state of affairs that is unjustifiable for lack of principle, and where there can only be disorder and confusion. This overthrow of all hierarchy begins as soon as temporal power wants to make itself independent of spiritual authority, then subordinate it by claiming to use it for political ends; This is the first usurpation that paves the way for all the others, and it could be shown that, for example, French royalty, since the fourteenth century, has itself unconsciously worked to prepare the Revolution that was to overthrow it; perhaps some day we'll have the opportunity to develop this point of view, which for the moment we can only outline in a very summary way.

If we define "democracy" as the government of the people by themselves, this is a real impossibility, something that cannot even have a simple existence in fact, any more in our time than in any other; We must not be fooled by words, and it is contradictory to admit that the same men can be both governors and governed at the same time, because, to use Aristotelian language, the same being cannot be "in act" and "in power" at the same time and in the same respect. This is a relationship that necessarily presupposes the presence of two terms: there could be no governed if there were not also governors, even if they were illegitimate and had no right to power other than that which they have attributed to themselves; but the great skill of rulers in the modern world is to make the people believe that they govern themselves; and the people allow themselves to be persuaded all the more readily because they are flattered by this, and because they are incapable of thinking hard enough to see what is impossible about it. Universal suffrage" was invented to create this illusion: it's the opinion of the majority that's supposed to make the law; but what we don't realize is that opinion is something that can very easily be directed and modified; we can always, with the help of appropriate suggestions, provoke currents in it going in this or that determined direction; we don't know who said that "opinion is manufactured", and this expression is quite accurate, although it must be said that it is not always the apparent leaders who actually have at their disposal the means necessary to obtain this result. This last remark undoubtedly explains why the incompetence of the most "prominent" politicians seems to be of only relative importance; but, as it is not our intention here to dismantle the workings of what might be called the "governing machine", we shall confine ourselves to pointing out that this very incompetence offers the advantage of maintaining the illusion we have just been talking about: it is only under these conditions, in fact, that the politicians in question can appear to be the emanation of the majority, being thus in its image, for the majority, on whatever subject it is called upon to give its opinion, is always made up of the incompetent, whose number is incomparably greater than that of the men who are capable of pronouncing themselves in full knowledge of the facts.

This immediately brings us to how the idea that the majority should make the law is essentially flawed, for even if this idea is, by necessity, mainly theoretical and cannot correspond to an actual reality, it remains to be explained how it has been able to implant itself in the modern mind, what are the tendencies of the latter to which it corresponds and which it satisfies, at least in appearance. The most obvious flaw is the one we mentioned earlier: the majority opinion can only be the expression of incompetence, whether this is the result of a lack of intelligence or pure and simple ignorance; in this respect, we could bring in certain observations of "collective psychology", and recall in particular the well-known fact that, in a crowd, the totality of mental reactions occurring between the component individuals leads to the formation of a kind of resultant which is not even at the level of the average, but at that of the most inferior elements. On the other hand, we should also note how certain modern philosophers have sought to transfer to the intellectual order the "democratic" theory that gives precedence to the opinion of the majority, by making what they call "universal consent" an alleged "criterion of truth" : even supposing there were indeed a question on which all men agreed, this agreement would prove nothing by itself ; but, moreover, if this unanimity really existed - which is all the more doubtful as there are always many men who have no opinion on any question, and who have never even asked themselves the question - it would in any case be impossible to ascertain it in fact, so that what is invoked in favour of an opinion and as a sign of its truth is reduced to being no more than the consent of the greatest number, and even then restricted to an environment necessarily very limited in space and time. In this field, it is even clearer that theory lacks a basis, because it is easier to avoid the influence of sentiment, which almost inevitably comes into play when it comes to politics; and it is this influence that is one of the main obstacles to understanding certain things, even in those who would otherwise have ample intellectual capacity to achieve this understanding without difficulty; emotional impulses prevent reflection, and it is one of the most vulgar skills of politics to take advantage of this incompatibility.

But let's get to the heart of the matter: what exactly is this law of the greatest number that modern governments invoke, and from which they claim to derive their sole justification? Quite simply, it's the law of matter and brute force, the very law by virtue of which a mass driven by its own weight crushes everything in its path; this is precisely where the "democratic" conception and "materialism" meet, and it's also what makes this same conception so closely linked to today's mentality. It's a complete reversal of the normal order, since it proclaims the supremacy of multiplicity as such, a supremacy which, in fact, exists only in the material world[2] ; on the contrary, in the spiritual world, and even more simply in the universal order, it is unity that is at the top of the hierarchy, for it is unity that is the principle from which all multiplicity emerges[3] ; but, when the principle is denied or lost sight of, all that remains is pure multiplicity, which is identified with matter itself. On the other hand, the allusion we've just made to gravity implies more than a simple comparison, for in the realm of physical forces in the most ordinary sense of the word, gravity actually represents the downward, compressive tendency that leads to ever-tighter limitation for being, and which at the same time moves in the direction of multiplicity, represented here by ever-increasing density[4] ; and this is the very trend that has marked the direction in which human activity has developed since the beginning of the modern era. Furthermore, it should be noted that matter, with its power to divide and limit at the same time, is what Scholastic doctrine calls the "principle of individuation", and this links the considerations we are now expounding to what we said earlier about individualism: the same tendency we've just been talking about is also, we might say, the "individualizing" tendency, that according to which what Judeo-Christian tradition designates as the "fall" of beings who have separated from the original unity[5] takes place. In the social order, the multiplicity considered outside its principle, and which can thus no longer be reduced to unity, is the collectivity conceived as simply the arithmetical sum of the individuals that make it up, and which is indeed just that, since it is not linked to any principle superior to individuals; and the law of the collectivity, in this respect, is indeed the law of the greatest number on which the "democratic" idea is based.

We need to stop here for a moment to clear up a possible confusion: in speaking of modern individualism, we have considered almost exclusively its manifestations in the intellectual order; one might think that, as far as the social order is concerned, the case is quite different. Indeed, if we were to take the word "individualism" in its narrowest sense, we might be tempted to oppose the collectivity to the individual, and to think that facts such as the increasingly invasive role of the State and the growing complexity of social institutions are the mark of a tendency contrary to individualism. In reality, this is not the case at all, for the collectivity, being nothing other than the sum of individuals, cannot be opposed to them, any more than the State itself, conceived in the modern way, i.e. as a simple representation of the mass, in which no higher principle is reflected; and it is precisely in the negation of any supra-individual principle that individualism, as we have defined it, truly consists. So, if there are conflicts in the social sphere between various tendencies, all of which belong equally to the modern spirit, these conflicts are not between individualism and something else, but simply between the multiple varieties of which individualism itself is susceptible ; and it is easy to see that, in the absence of any principle capable of truly unifying multiplicity, such conflicts must be more numerous and more serious in our time than they have ever been, for individualism necessarily means division; and this division, with the chaotic state it engenders, is the fatal consequence of an all-material civilization, since it is matter itself that is properly the root of division and multiplicity.

It's not for nothing that "democracy" is opposed to "aristocracy", the latter precisely designating, at least in its etymological sense, the power of the elite. By definition, this elite can only be the few, and its power - or rather, its authority, which derives solely from its intellectual superiority - has nothing in common with the numerical force on which "democracy" is based, whose essential character is to sacrifice the minority to the majority, and thus, as we said earlier, quality to quantity, i.e. the elite to the masses. Thus, the guiding role of a true elite, and its very existence - for it necessarily plays this role as soon as it exists - are radically incompatible with "democracy", which is intimately linked to the "egalitarian" conception, i.e. to the negation of all hierarchy: the very basis of the "democratic" idea is that any individual is worth another, because they are numerically equal, even though they can only ever be numerically equal. A true elite, as we've already said, can only be intellectual; that's why "democracy" can only be established where pure intellectuality no longer exists, which is effectively the case in the modern world. However, as equality is impossible in practice, and as it is practically impossible to eliminate all differences between men, despite all efforts at levelling, we end up, by a curious illogicality, inventing false elites, of which there are many, which claim to replace the only real elite; and these false elites are based on the consideration of some kind of superiority, eminently relative and contingent, and always of a purely material nature. We can easily see this by noting that the social distinction that counts most in the present state of affairs is that based on wealth, i.e. on a superiority that is entirely external and exclusively quantitative, the only one in fact that can be reconciled with "democracy", because it proceeds from the same point of view. We would add, moreover, that the very people who are currently posing as opponents of this state of affairs, and who do not call upon any principle of a higher order, are incapable of effectively remedying such disorder, if they do not even risk aggravating it by going further and further in the same direction; the struggle is only between varieties of "democracy", accentuating more or less the "egalitarian" tendency, as it is, as we have said, between varieties of individualism, which, moreover, amounts to exactly the same thing.

These few reflections seem to us sufficient to characterize the social state of the contemporary world, and to show at the same time that, in this field as in all others, there can be only one way out of chaos: the restoration of intellectuality and, consequently, the reconstitution of an elite, which, at present, must be regarded as non-existent in the West, because we cannot give this name to a few isolated and un-cohesive elements, which represent, as it were, only undeveloped possibilities. In fact, these elements generally only have tendencies or aspirations, which no doubt lead them to react against the modern spirit, but without being able to exert their influence in an effective way; what they lack is true knowledge, traditional data which cannot be impro-vised, and which an intelligence left to its own devices, es-pecially in such unfavorable circumstances in every respect, can only make up for very imperfectly and to a very small extent. The modern world defends itself by its own disper-sion, from which its adversaries themselves are unable to es-cape. This will be the case for as long as they remain on the "profane" terrain, where the modern spirit has an obvious ad-vantage, since this is its own and exclusive domain; and, moreover, if they remain there, it's because this spirit still has a very strong hold on them, despite everything. This is why so many people, despite their unquestionable good will, are incapable of understanding that we must necessarily start with principles, and insist on wasting their strength in this or that relative field, social or otherwise, where nothing real or lasting can be achieved under these conditions. The true elite, on the other hand, would have no need to intervene di-rectly in these fields, nor to become involved in external ac-tion; it would direct everything through an influence that would be elusive to the vulgar, and all the more profound for being less apparent. If we think of the power of the sugges-tions we spoke of earlier, and which nevertheless presuppose no real intellectuality, we can suspect what would be, a for-tiori, the power of an influence like this, exerting itself in an even more hidden way due to its very nature, This power, moreover, instead of being diminished by the division inhe-rent in multiplicity, and by the weakness inherent in all that is falsehood or illusion, would on the contrary be intensified by concentration in principial unity, and would become iden-tified with the very force of truth.

1 - What men call chance is simply their ignorance of causes; if, by saying that something happens by chance, we were to imply that there is no cause, this would be a self-contradictory supposition.

2 - You only have to read Saint Thomas Aquinas to see that "*numerus stat ex parte materiae*".

3 - From one order of reality to another, the analogy, here as in all similar cases, applies strictly in reverse.

4 - This tendency is what Hindu doctrine calls *tamas*, and equates it with ignorance and obscurity: it should be noted that, in line with what we said earlier about the application of analogy, the compression or condensation in question is the opposite of the concentration envisaged in the spiritual or intellectual order, so that, strange as it may seem at first, it is in fact correlative to division and dispersion in multiplicity. The same is true of the uniformity achieved from below, at the most inferior level, according to the "egalitarian" conception, and which is the extreme opposite of superior, principial unity.

5 - This is why Dante places Lucifer's symbolic abode at the center of the earth, i.e. at the point where the forces of gravity converge on all sides; this is, in this respect, the opposite of the center of spiritual or "celestial" attraction, which is symbolized by the sun in most traditional doctrines.

CHAPTER VII

A MATERIAL CIVILIZATION

From all the foregoing, it seems clear to us that the Orientals are quite right when they criticize modern Western civilization for being all material: it is indeed in this sense that it has developed exclusively, and, from whatever point of view we consider it, we always find ourselves in the presence of the more or less direct consequences of this materialization. However, we still need to complete what we have said in this respect, and first of all to explain the different meanings in which a word like "materialism" can be taken, because if we use it to characterize the contemporary world, some people who don't believe themselves to be "materialists" at all, while claiming to be very "modern", will not fail to protest and persuade themselves that this is a real slander; A clarification is therefore necessary to rule out any misunderstandings that may arise on this subject.

Significantly enough, the very word "materialism" dates back only to the eighteenth century, when it was coined by the philosopher Berkeley to designate any theory that admits the real existence of matter; needless to say, that's not what we're talking about here, where such existence is in no way in question. A little later, the same word took on a more restricted meaning, the one it has retained ever since: it characterizes a conception according to which nothing exists other than matter and what proceeds from it; and it is worth noting the novelty of such a conception, the fact that it is essentially a product of the modern mind, and thus corresponds to at least part of the tendencies that are peculiar to it[1]. But it is above all in another, much broader and yet very clear, sense that we mean here by "materialism": what this word represents is a whole state of mind, of which the conception we have just defined is only one manifestation among many others, and which is, in itself, independent of any philosophical theory. This state of mind is that which consists in more or less consciously giving precedence to things of the material order and to preoccupations related to them, whether these preoccupations still retain a certain speculative appearance or are purely practical; and it cannot be seriously contested that this is indeed the mentality of the vast majority of our contemporaries.

All the "profane" science that has developed over the last few centuries is the study of the sensible world, confined exclusively to it, and its methods are applicable to this domain alone; yet these methods are proclaimed to be "scientific" to the exclusion of all others, which amounts to denying any science that does not relate to material things. Among those who think in this way, and even among those who have devoted themselves specifically to the sciences in question, there are nevertheless many who would refuse to declare themselves "materialists" and adhere to the philosophical theory that bears this name; there are even those who willingly make a profession of religious faith whose sincerity is not in doubt; but their "scientific" attitude does not differ appreciably from that of avowed materialists. From a religious point of view, the question of whether modern science should be denounced as atheistic or materialistic has often been debated, and more often than not it has been badly put. It is quite certain that this science does not expressly profess atheism or materialism, that it limits itself to ignoring certain things out of bias, without pronouncing itself on them by a formal negation, as some philosophers do; As far as it's concerned, then, we can only speak of a de facto materialism, of what we would gladly call a practical materialism; but the evil is perhaps all the more serious, because it's deeper and more widespread. A philosophical attitude can be something very superficial, even among "professional" philosophers; moreover, there are minds that would recoil at negation, but are content with complete indifference; and this is what is most dreadful, for, to deny a thing, you still have to think about it, however little, whereas here we come to think about it no more in any way. When we see an exclusively material science presented as the only possible science, when men are accustomed to admitting as an indisputable truth that there can be no valid knowledge outside of it, when all the education they are given tends to inculcate in them the superstition of this science, which is properly "scientism", how could these men not be practically materialistic, i.e. not have all their preoccupations turned to the side of matter?

For modern people, nothing seems to exist beyond what can be seen and touched, or at least, even if they admit theoretically that something else may exist, they are quick to declare it not only unknown, but "unknowable", which dispenses them from dealing with it. If, however, there are those who seek to form some idea of an "other world", as they do so only through the imagination, they represent it on the model of the terrestrial world, transporting into it all the conditions of existence that are proper to the latter, including space and time, and even a kind of "corporeality"; But if this is an extreme case, where this character is exaggerated to the point of caricature, it would be a mistake to believe that Spiritism and its more or less related sects have a monopoly on this sort of thing. On a more general note, the intervention of the imagination in domains where it can give nothing, and which should normally be forbidden to it, is a fact which clearly shows the inability of modern Westerners to rise above the sensible; many cannot distinguish between "conceive" and "imagine", and some philosophers, such as Kant, go so far as to declare "inconceivable" or "unthinkable" anything that is not susceptible of representation. So what we call "spiritualism" or "idealism" is, more often than not, no more than a kind of transposed materialism; this is true not only of what we have called "neo-spiritualism", but also of philosophical spiritualism itself, which considers itself to be the opposite of materialism. In fact, spiritualism and materialism, understood in the philosophical sense, cannot be understood without each other: they are simply the two halves of Cartesian dualism, whose radical separation has been transformed into a kind of antagonism; and, since then, all philosophy has oscillated between these two terms without being able to overcome them. Spiritualism, despite its name, has nothing in common with spirituality; its debate with materialism can only leave those who take a higher viewpoint completely indifferent, and who see that these opposites are, at bottom, very close to being mere equivalents, whose supposed opposition, on many points, is reduced to a vulgar dispute over words.

Moderns, in general, conceive of no science other than that of things that can be measured, counted and weighed, i.e., in short, material things, for it is only to these that the quantitative point of view can be applied; and the claim to reduce quality to quantity is very characteristic of modern science. In this sense, we have come to believe that there is no science as such where it is not possible to introduce measurement, and that scientific laws are only those that express quantitative relationships; Descartes' "mechanism" marked the beginning of this tendency, which has only become more pronounced since then, despite the failure of Cartesian physics, because it is not linked to a specific theory, but to a general conception of scientific knowledge. Today, we want to apply measurement even in the psychological domain, which by its very nature escapes it; we end up no longer understanding that the possibility of measurement rests solely on a property inherent in matter, and which is its indefinite divisibility, unless we think that this property extends to everything that exists, which amounts to materializing all things. As we have already said, it is matter that is the principle of division and pure multiplicity; the predominance attributed to the point of view of quantity, and which, as we have already shown, can be found even in the social domain, is therefore indeed materialism in the sense we indicated above, although it is not necessarily linked to philosophical materialism, which, moreover, it preceded in the development of the tendencies of the modern mind. We shall not insist on the illegitimacy of reducing quality to quantity, nor on the inadequacy of all attempts at explanation that are more or less of the "mechanistic" type; this is not our purpose, and we shall only note in this respect that, even in the sensible order, a science of this kind has very little to do with reality, the most considerable part of which necessarily escapes it.

On the subject of "reality", we'd like to mention another fact, which may go unnoticed by many, but which is highly noteworthy as a sign of the state of mind we're talking about: it's that this name, in common usage, is reserved exclusively for sensible reality. As language is the expression of the mentality of a people and an era, we must conclude that, for those who speak in this way, anything that does not fall within the realm of the senses is "unreal", i.e. illusory or even completely non-existent; They may not be clearly aware of this, but this negative conviction is nonetheless deep within them, and if they assert the contrary, we can be sure, even if they don't realize it, that this assertion only responds in them to something much more external, if not purely verbal. If you're tempted to think we're exaggerating, just look at what many people's so-called religious convictions boil down to: A few notions learned by heart, in a very scholastic and mechanical way, which they have in no way assimilated, to which they have never even given the slightest thought, but which they keep in their memory and repeat on occasion because they are part of a certain formalism, a conventional attitude which is all they can understand under the name of religion. We have already spoken of this "minimization" of religion, of which the "verbalism" in question represents one of the last degrees; it is this that explains why so-called "believers", in terms of practical materialism, yield nothing to "unbelievers"; we will return to this point later, but first we must   conclude   our   considerations   concerning   the materialistic character of modern science, for this is a question that needs to be considered from different angles.

As we have already pointed out, modern science is not a disinterested form of knowledge, and even for those who believe in its speculative value, it is little more than a mask for practical preoccupations, allowing them to maintain the illusion of a false intellectuality. Descartes himself, in building up his physics, was thinking above all of deriving mechanics, medicine and morals from it; and, with the spread of empiricism in the Anglo-Saxon world, it was something else again; besides, what makes science prestigious in the eyes of the general public is almost exclusively the practical results it achieves, because here again, we're talking about things that can be seen and touched. We have said that "pragmatism" represents the culmination of all modern philosophy and its final degree of debasement; but there is also, and has been for longer, a diffuse and unsystematized "pragmatism" outside philosophy, which is to the other what practical materialism is to theoretical materialism, and which merges with what the vulgar call "common sense". This almost instinctive utilitarianism is, moreover, inseparable from the materialist tendency: for him, "common sense" means not going beyond the earthly horizon, and not caring about anything that is not of immediate practical interest; above all, it means that the sensible world alone is "real", and that there is no knowledge that does not come from the senses; For him, too, this restricted knowledge is only worthwhile insofar as it allows us to satisfy material needs, and sometimes a certain sentimentalism, for - it must be said clearly, at the risk of shocking contemporary "moralism" - sentiment is in reality very close to matter. In all this, there is no place left for intelligence, except insofar as it consents to be enslaved to the achievement of practical ends, to be no more than a mere instrument subject to the demands of the lower, bodily part of the human individual, or, to borrow a singular expression from Bergson, "a tool for making tools"; what makes "pragmatism" in all its forms is a total indifference to truth.

Under these conditions, industry is no longer simply an application of science, from which science itself should be totally independent at ; it becomes its raison d'être and justification, so that, here again, normal relationships are reversed. What the modern world has applied all its energies to, even when it has pretended to do science its own way, is in reality nothing other than the development of industry and "machinismo"; and, in thus wishing to dominate matter and bend it to their use, men have only succeeded in making slaves of it, as we said at the beginning: not only have they limited their intellectual ambitions - if we can still use the word in such cases - to inventing and building machines, but they have ended up becoming true machines themselves. Indeed, "specialization", so extolled by some sociologists under the name of "division of labor", has imposed itself not only on scientists, but also on technicians and even workers, making intelligent work impossible for the latter; They have to repeat incessantly, in a completely mechanical way, certain specific movements, always the same, and always performed in the same way, to avoid wasting the slightest amount of time; at least, this is how the American methods, which are considered to represent the highest degree of "progress", want it. Once again, we come back to the same observation we've already made in other areas: modern civilization is really what you might call a quantitative civilization, which is just another way of saying that it's a material civilization.

If we wish to be even more convinced of this truth, we need only look at the immense role played today, in the existence of peoples as well as individuals, by economic elements: industry, commerce, finance, it seems that these are the only things that count, which is in line with the fact already pointed out that the only social distinction that has survived is that based on material wealth. It seems that financial power dominates all politics, that commercial competition exerts a preponderant influence on relations between peoples; perhaps this is only an appearance, and these things are here less real causes than mere means of action; but the choice of such means does indicate the character of the age to which they are suited. What's more, our contemporaries are convinced that economic circumstances are more or less the only factors in historical events, and they even imagine that this has always been the case; they have gone so far as to invent a theory that seeks to explain everything exclusively in this way, and which has been given the significant appellation of "historical materialism". Here again, we can see the effect of one of those suggestions to which we alluded earlier, suggestions which are all the more effective as they correspond to the tendencies of the general mentality; and the effect of this suggestion is that economic means end up really determining almost everything that happens in the social sphere. Without doubt, the masses have always been led in one way or another, and it could be said that their historical role consists above all in allowing themselves to be led, because they represent only a passive element, a "matter" in the Aristotelian sense ; but today, to lead it, it is enough to have purely material means at one's disposal, this time in the ordinary sense of the word, which clearly shows the degree of debasement of our times; and, at the same time, this mass is made to believe that it is not led, that it acts spontaneously and governs itself, and the fact that it believes this gives us a glimpse of how far its unintelligence can go.

While we're on the subject of economic factors, we'd like to take this opportunity to point out an all-too-common delusion on this subject, which consists in imagining that relations established in the field of trade can serve to bring peoples closer together and foster understanding, when in reality they have exactly the opposite effect. As we've said many times before, matter is essentially multiplicity and division, and therefore a source of struggle and conflict. So, whether we're talking about peoples or individuals, the economic sphere is and can only be one of rivalry of interests. In particular, the West does not have to rely on industry, nor on the modern science of which it is an inseparable part, to find common ground with the East; if the Orientals come to accept this industry as an unfortunate and moreover transitory necessity, because for them it can be nothing more than that, it will only ever be as a weapon enabling them to resist Western encroachment and safeguard their own existence. It is important to realize that it cannot be otherwise: Orientals who resign themselves to considering economic competition with the West, despite their repugnance for this kind of activity, can only do so with one intention in mind: to rid themselves of a foreign domination that relies solely on brute force, on the material power that industry places precisely at its disposal; violence calls for violence, but we must recognize that it is certainly not Orientals who will have sought the struggle on this terrain.

Leaving aside the question of the relationship between East and West, it's easy to see that one of the most notable consequences of industrial development is the ceaseless improvement of war machines and the increase in their destructive power to formidable proportions. But dreamers and idealists are incorrigible, and their naivety seems to know no bounds. The "humanitarianism" that is so much in vogue certainly doesn't deserve to be taken seriously; but it's strange that there's so much talk of the end of wars at a time when they are wreaking more havoc than ever before, not only because of the multiplication of the means of destruction, but also because, instead of taking place between small armies composed solely of professional soldiers, they throw all individuals indiscriminately against each other, including those least qualified to perform such a function. This is another striking example of modern confusion, and it is truly amazing, if you think about it, that we have come to regard a "levée en masse" or "mobilization en masse" as a matter of course, that the idea of an "armed nation" has been able to impose itself on all minds, with very few exceptions. This may also be seen as an effect of the belief in the power of numbers alone: it's in keeping with the quantitative character of modern civilization to set huge masses of combatants in motion; and, at the same time, "egalitarianism" is well served by this, as well as by institutions such as "compulsory education" and "universal suffrage". Let us add that these generalized wars were only made possible by another specifically modern phenomenon, namely the constitution of "nationalities", the consequence of the destruction of the feudal regime, on the one hand, and, on the other, of the simultaneous rupture of the superior unity of the "Christendom" of the Middle Ages; And, without going into too much detail, we should also note, as an aggravating circumstance, the disregard for a spiritual authority which alone can normally exercise effective arbitration, because it is, by its very nature, above all political conflicts. The denial of spiritual authority is still practical materialism; and the very people who claim to recognize such authority in principle are in fact denying it any real influence and any power to intervene in the social sphere, in exactly the same way as they establish a watertight partition between religion and the ordinary concerns of their existence; whether in public or private life, it's the same state of mind that asserts itself in both cases.

Admitting that material development has some advantages, albeit from a very relative point of view, when we consider consequences such as those we have just mentioned, we may well wonder whether these advantages are not far outweighed by the disadvantages. We're not even talking about all that has been sacrificed to this exclusive development, which was worth incomparably more; we're not talking about forgotten higher knowledge, destroyed intellectuality, vanished spirituality; we're simply taking modern civilization in itself, and saying that, if we were to compare the advantages and disadvantages of what it has produced, the result would very likely be negative. The inventions that are currently multiplying with ever-increasing speed are all the more dangerous because they bring into play forces whose true nature is entirely unknown to the very people who use them; and this ignorance is the best proof of the nullity of modern science in terms of explanatory value, i.e. as knowledge, even if restricted to the physical domain alone; at the same time, the fact that practical applications are in no way prevented by this shows that this science is indeed oriented solely in a self-interested direction, that industry is the only real goal of all its research. As the danger of inventions, even those which are not expressly intended to play a disastrous role for mankind, and which nonetheless cause so many disasters, not to mention the unsuspected disturbances they provoke in the earth's atmosphere, as this danger, we say, will undoubtedly continue to increase in proportions that are difficult to determine, it is reasonable to think, without too much implausibility, as we have already indicated, that it is perhaps in this way that the modern world will come to destroy itself, if it is incapable of stopping along this path while there is still time.

But it's not enough to make the necessary reservations about modern inventions, because of their dangerous side, and we need to go further: aren't the so-called "benefits" of what is commonly called "progress" - and which we could indeed agree to designate as such, if we were careful to specify that it's only a question of purely material progress - largely illusory? The men of our time claim to be increasing their "well-being"; for our part, we think that the goal they set themselves, even if it were really achieved, is not worth the effort; but, what's more, it seems highly questionable whether it will be achieved at all. First of all, we need to take into account the fact that not all men have the same tastes or the same needs, and that there are still some who would like to escape modern agitation, the madness of speed, and who can no longer do so; do we dare argue that, for these people, it is a "blessing" to impose on them what is most contrary to their nature? As in the political sphere, the majority arrogates to itself the right to crush minorities, who, in its eyes, are obviously wrong to exist, since their very existence runs counter to the "egalitarian" mania for uniformity. But if we consider humanity as a whole, rather than just the Western world, the question changes: won't the majority just now become a minority? It is no longer the same argument that is put forward in this case, and, by a strange contradiction, it is in the name of their "superiority" that these "egalitarians" want to impose their civilization on the rest of the world, and that they are going to stir up trouble among people who asked nothing of them; and, as this "superiority" exists only from a material point of view, it is only natural that it should be imposed by the most brutal means. Make no mistake about it: while the general public accepts in good faith these pretexts of "civilization", there are some for whom it's nothing more than "moralist" hypocrisy, a mask for the spirit of conquest and economic interests; but what a peculiar time it is, when so many men allow themselves to be persuaded that the happiness of a people is achieved by enslaving it, by taking from it what it holds most precious, namely its own civilization, by forcing it to adopt mores and institutions that are made for another race, and by forcing it to do the most arduous work in order to make it acquire things that are of the most perfect uselessness to it! For this is how it is: the modern West cannot tolerate the fact that people prefer to work less and make do with little in order to live. Since quantity alone counts, and since what does not fall under the senses is moreover considered non-existent, it is accepted that anyone who is not restless and who does not produce materially can only be "lazy"; without even mentioning in this respect the assessments commonly made of Eastern peoples, one only has to look at how contemplative orders are judged, even in so-called religious circles. In such a world, there is no room for intelligence or for anything purely interior, for these are things that cannot be seen or touched, counted or weighed; there is only room for external action in all its forms, including the most meaningless. It's no wonder, then, that the Anglo-Saxon mania for "sport" is gaining ground by the day: the ideal of this world is the "human animal" who has developed his muscular strength to the utmost; its heroes are athletes, even if they are brutes; it's these who arouse popular enthusiasm, it's for their exploits that the crowds are enthralled; a world where such things are seen has truly fallen very low and seems very close to its end.

But let's consider for a moment the point of view of those who place their ideal in material "well-being", and who, as such, rejoice in all the improvements brought to existence by modern "progress". Are they quite sure they're not being fooled? Is it true that people are happier today than in the past, because they have faster means of communication or other such things, because their lives are more hectic and complicated? It seems to us that the opposite is true: imbalance cannot be the condition of true happiness ; besides, the more needs a man has, the more likely he is to lack something, and therefore to be unhappy; modern civilization aims to multiply artificial needs, and, as we said earlier, it will always create more needs than it can satisfy, because once you've started down this road, it's very difficult to stop, and there's no reason to stop at any particular point. Men couldn't suffer for being deprived of things that didn't exist and that they'd never thought about; now, on the contrary, they must suffer if they lack these things, since they've become accustomed to seeing them as necessary, and in fact they have become necessary. So they do everything in their power to acquire the only material satisfactions they are capable of appreciating: it's all about "making money", because that's what it takes to get these things, and the more you have, the more you want, because you're constantly discovering new needs; and this passion becomes the sole aim of your whole life. Hence the fierce competition that some "evolutionists" have elevated to the dignity of a scientific law under the name of the "struggle for life", the logical consequence of which is that the strongest, in the most narrowly material sense of the word, have the sole right to existence. Hence also the envy and even hatred of those who possess wealth on the part of those who lack it; how can men who have been preached to about "egalitarian" theories fail to revolt when they see inequality all around them in the form that must be most sensitive to them, because it is of the crudest order? If modern civilization were to collapse one day under the pressure of the disordered appetites it has aroused in the masses, one would have to be very blind not to see in it the just punishment of its fundamental vice, or, to put it without any moral phraseology, the "backlash" of its own action in the very field where it has been exercised. It is said in the Gospel: "He who strikes with the sword will perish by the sword"; he who unleashes the brutal forces of matter will perish crushed by these same forces, of which he is no longer master once he has recklessly set them in motion, and which he cannot boast of holding back indefinitely in their fatal march; It doesn't matter whether the forces of nature or the forces of the human masses, or all of them together, it's always the laws of matter that come into play and inexorably shatter the man who thought he could dominate them without himself rising above matter. And the Gospel goes on to say: "Every house divided against itself will fall"; this word also applies exactly to the modern world, with its material civilization, which by its very nature can only give rise to struggle and division everywhere. The conclusion is too easy to draw, and there is no need to appeal to other considerations to be able, without fear of being wrong, to predict a tragic end for this world, unless a radical change, even to the point of a real reversal, takes place in the near future.

We are well aware that some will reproach us for having, in speaking of the materialism of modern civilization as we have just done, neglected certain elements which seem to constitute at least an attenuation of this materialism; and indeed, if there were none, it is highly probable that this civilization would already have perished lamentably. We do not dispute the existence of such elements, but we must not delude ourselves: on the one hand, we don't have to include everything that, in the philosophical realm, is presented under labels like "spiritualism" and "idealism", nor everything that, in contemporary trends, is nothing but "moralism" and "sentimentalism"; On the other hand, if there are still remnants of true spirituality, it is in spite of and against the modern spirit that they have survived to date. These remnants of spirituality can only be found, in the case of everything that is properly Western, in the religious order; but we have already said how much religion has been watered down today, how narrow and mediocre its followers themselves think it is, and to what extent the intellectuality that is one with true spirituality has been eliminated; In these conditions, if certain possibilities still remain, they are barely latent, and in the present, their actual role is reduced to very little. Nevertheless, we must admire the vitality of a religious tradition which, even when reduced to a kind of virtuality, persists despite all the efforts that have been made over the centuries to stifle and annihilate it; But, once again, this tradition does not belong to the modern world, it is not one of its constituent elements, it is the very opposite of its tendencies and aspirations. We must be frank about this, and not seek vain reconciliations: between the religious spirit, in the true sense of the word, and the modern spirit, there can only be antagonism; any compromise can only weaken the former and benefit the latter, whose hostility will not be disarmed because it can only seek the complete destruction of everything in humanity that reflects a reality superior to humanity.

It is said that the modern West is Christian, but this is a mistake: the modern mind is anti-Christian, because it is essentially anti-religious; and it is anti-religious because, more generally still, it is anti-traditional; this is what constitutes its own character, what makes it what it is. Certainly, something of Christianity has passed into the anti-Christian civilization of our time, whose most "advanced" representatives, as they say in their special language, cannot help but have undergone and still undergo, involuntarily and perhaps unconsciously, a certain Christian influence, at least indirectly; this is so because a break with the past, however radical, can never be absolutely complete and such as to do away with all continuity. We would go even further, and say that all that is valid in the modern world has come to it from Christianity, or at least through Christianity, which brought with it all the heritage of earlier traditions, which has kept it alive as far as the state of the West has allowed, and which still carries within itself the latent possibilities; but who today, even among those who claim to be Christians, is still effectively aware of these possibilities? Where, even in Catholicism, are the men who know the deeper meaning of the doctrine they profess outwardly, who are not content to "believe" in a more or less superficial way, and more by feeling than by intelligence, but who really "know" the truth of the religious tradition they consider their own? We would like to have proof that at least some of them exist, for this would be, for the West, the greatest and perhaps the only hope of salvation; but we must confess that, so far, we have not yet met any; must we suppose that, like certain sages of the East, they are hidden away in some almost inaccessible retreat, or must we definitively renounce this last hope? The West was Christian in the Middle Ages, but it is no longer so; if it is said that it can still become so again, no one hopes more than we do that this will be the case, and that it will happen on a day closer than anything we see around us would lead us to believe, but make no mistake: on that day, the modern world will have lived.

---

1 - Before the eighteenth century, there were "mechanistic" theories, from Greek atomism to Cartesian physics; but "mechanism" and "materialism" should not be confused, despite certain affinities that have created a kind of de facto solidarity between the two since the appearance of "materialism" proper.

CHAPTER VIII

WESTERN ENCROACHMENT

Modern disorder, as we have said, originated in the West, and until recent years had always remained strictly localized there; but now something is happening whose gravity must not be concealed: this disorder is spreading everywhere, and seems to be reaching as far as the East. Of course, Western encroachment is not a recent phenomenon, but until now it has been limited to a more or less brutal domination of other peoples, the effects of which have been confined to the political and economic sphere. Despite the best efforts of propaganda in many forms, the Eastern spirit was impenetrable to all deviations, and ancient traditional civilizations remained intact. Today, on the contrary, there are Orientals who have become more or less completely "Westernized", who have abandoned their tradition to adopt all the aberrations of the modern mind, and these deviated elements, thanks to the teaching of European and American universities, are becoming a cause of trouble and unrest in their own country. It would be wrong to exaggerate their importance, for the time being at least: In the West, we readily imagine that these noisy but few individualities represent the Orient of today, whereas in reality their action is neither very extensive nor very profound; this illusion is easily explained, for we don't know the real Orientals, who in any case make no attempt to make themselves known, and the "modernists", if we can call them that, are the only ones who show themselves to the outside world, speak, write and agitate in any case. Nevertheless, it is true that this anti-traditional movement may gain ground, and we must envisage all eventualities, even the most unfavorable; already, the traditional spirit is turning in on itself, and the centers where it is preserved in its entirety are becoming more and more closed and difficult to access; and this generalization of disorder corresponds well to what must occur in the final phase of the *Kali-Yuga*.

Let's state it very clearly: since the modern spirit is a purely Western thing, those who are affected by it, even if they are born Orientals, must be considered, in terms of mentality, as Westerners, since all Eastern ideas are entirely foreign to them, and their ignorance of traditional doctrines is the only excuse for their hostility. What may seem rather singular and even contradictory is that these same men, who make themselves the auxiliaries of "occidentalism" from the intellectual point of view, or more exactly against all true intellectuality, sometimes appear as its adversaries in the political field; and yet, deep down, there is nothing to be surprised about. It is they who are striving to institute various "nationalisms" in the East, and any "nationalism" is necessarily opposed to the traditional spirit; if they want to fight foreign domination, it is by the very methods of the West, in the same way as the various Western peoples fight among themselves; and perhaps this is what makes them so special. Indeed, if things have reached such a point that the use of such methods has become inevitable, their implementation can only be the work of elements who have severed all ties with tradition; it is therefore possible that these elements will be used in this way temporarily, and then eliminated like the Westerners themselves. Moreover, it would be quite logical for the ideas they have spread to be turned against them, as they can only be factors of division and ruin; this is how modern civilization will perish in one way or another; whether this is due to dissension among Westerners, between nations or social classes, or, as some claim, to attacks from "Westernized" Orientals, or to a cataclysm brought about by "scientific progress"; in any case, the Western world is in danger only through its own fault and through what comes out of itself.

The only question is this: will the modern mind cause the East to undergo only a fleeting, superficial crisis, or will the West drag down the whole of humanity? It would be difficult at present to provide an answer based on unmistakable facts; the two opposing spirits now exist in the East, and the spiritual force, inherent in the tradition and ignored by its adversaries, can triumph over the material force once the latter has played its part, and make it vanish as light dispels darkness; We would even go so far as to say that it will necessarily triumph sooner or later, but there may be a period of complete obscurity before this happens. The traditional spirit cannot die, because it is, in its essence, superior to death and change; but it can withdraw entirely from the outside world, and then it will truly be the "end of a world". From all that we have said, the realization of this eventuality in the relatively near future would not be implausible; and, in the confusion that is now spreading from the West to the East, we could see the "beginning of the end", the harbinger of the moment when, according to Hindu tradition, the sacred doctrine must be locked up in its entirety in a conch shell, to emerge intact at the dawn of the new world.

What is indisputable is that the West is invading everything; its action was first exercised in the material domain, that which was immediately within its reach, either through violent conquest, or through trade and the monopolization of all peoples' resources; but now things are going even further. Westerners, still driven by their particular need to proselytize, have succeeded in making their anti-traditional, materialistic spirit penetrate others to a certain extent; and whereas the first form of encroachment only affected bodies, this one is poisoning minds and killing spirituality; The one, moreover, prepared the other and made it possible, so that it is ultimately only by brute force that the West has succeeded in imposing itself everywhere, and it could not have been otherwise, for it is in this that lies the only real superiority of its civilization, so inferior in every other respect. The encroachment of the West is the encroachment of materialism in all its forms, and that's all it can be; All the more or less hypocritical disguises, all the "moralist" pretexts, all the "humanitarian" declamations, all the skills of a propaganda which occasionally knows how to be insinuating in order to better achieve its goal of destruction, can do nothing against this truth, which can only be contested by the naive or by those who have some interest in this truly "satanic" work, in the most rigorous sense of the word[1].

What is this new aberration? Despite our desire to confine ourselves to general considerations, we cannot refrain from saying at least a few words here about a recently published *Défense de l'Occident* by Henri Massis, which is one of the most characteristic manifestations of this state of mind. The book is full of confusions and even contradictions, and shows once again how little most of those who would like to react against modern disorder are capable of doing so in a truly effective way, because they don't even know very well what they have to fight against. The author sometimes defends himself from having set out to attack the real East; and, if he had indeed confined himself to a critique of "pseudo-Oriental" fantasies, i.e. of those purely Western theories that are being spread under misleading labels, and which are only one of the many products of the current imbalance, we could only fully approve of him, all the more so as we ourselves have pointed out, long before him, the real danger of these kinds of things, as well as their inanity from an intellectual point of view. But, unfortunately, he then feels the need to attribute to the East conceptions that are hardly any better than these; to do so, he relies on quotations borrowed from a few more or less "official" orientalists, and in which Oriental doctrines are, as is usually the case, distorted to the point of caricature; what would he say if someone used the same procedure with regard to Christianity and claimed to judge it according to the works of academic "hypercritics"? This is exactly what he does for the doctrines of India and China, with the aggravating circumstance that the Westerners whose testimony he invokes have not the slightest direct knowledge of these doctrines, while those of their colleagues who deal with Christianity must at least know it to some extent, even if their hostility to all things religious prevents them from truly understanding it. Moreover, we have to say on this occasion that we have sometimes had some difficulty in getting Orientals to admit that the presentations of such and such an Orientalist stemmed from a pure and simple lack of understanding, and not from a conscious and voluntary bias, so much so that one senses in them the same hostility which is inherent in the anti-traditional spirit; and we would gladly ask Massis whether he thinks it very skilful to attack tradition in others when one would like to restore it in one's own country. We say "clever" because, basically, the whole discussion is being carried on by him on a political terrain; for us, who take a completely different point of view, that of pure intellectuality, the only question that arises is one of truth; but this point of view is undoubtedly too elevated and too serene for polemicists to find satisfaction in it, and we even doubt that, as polemicists, concern for truth can hold a high place in their preoccupations[2].

Massis is attacking what he calls "Eastern propagandists", an expression which in itself contains a contradiction, for the spirit of propaganda, as we have often said, is an entirely Western thing, and this alone clearly indicates that there is some misunderstanding here. In fact, among the propagandists in question, we can distinguish two groups, the first of which is made up of pure Westerners; it would be truly comical, were it not for the sign of the most deplorable ignorance of things Eastern, to see that Germans and Russians are included among the representatives of the Eastern spirit; the author makes observations about them, some of which are very accurate, but why doesn't he show them clearly for what they really are? To this first group we would add the Anglo-Saxon "theosophists" and all the inventors of other sects of the same kind, whose Oriental terminology is no more than a mask designed to impose it on the naive and uninformed, and which covers only ideas as foreign to the East as they are dear to the modern West; these are more dangerous than mere philosophers, because of their claims to an "esotericism" which they don't possess either, but which they fraudulently simulate in order to attract to them minds that are looking for something other than "profane" speculations and which, in the midst of the present chaos, don't know where to turn; we are a little surprised that Massis doesn't say much about this. Massis has little to say about this. As for the second group, we find here some of those Westernized Orientals we spoke of earlier, who, just as ignorant as the previous of true Oriental ideas, would be quite incapable of spreading them in the West, supposing they had any intention of doing so; Moreover, their real aim is quite the opposite, since it is to destroy these same ideas in the East, and at the same time to present to Westerners their modernized East, accommodated to the theories taught to them in Europe or America; true agents of the most harmful of all Western propaganda, that which directly attacks the intelligence, it is for the East that they are a danger, and not for the West, of which they are only a reflection. As for real Orientals, Massis doesn't mention a single one, and he would have been hard-pressed to do so, as he certainly doesn't know any; the impossibility of naming a non-Westernized Oriental should have given him pause for thought and made him realize that "Oriental propagandists" are completely non-existent.

Moreover, although this forces us to talk about ourselves, which is not our custom, we must formally declare the following: to the best of our knowledge, no one has ever expounded authentic Eastern ideas in the West, except ourselves; and we have always done so in exactly the same way as any Oriental who has been led to do so by circumstances, i.e. without the slightest intention of "propaganda" or "popularization", and solely for those who are capable of understanding the doctrines as they are, without any need to distort them on the pretext of making them accessible to them; and we would add that, despite the decline of Western intellectuality, those who do understand are even less rare than we would have supposed, though obviously only a small minority. Such an undertaking is certainly not of kind Massis imagines. Massis imagines, we dare not say for the sake of his cause, although the political nature of his book may authorize such an expression; Let us say, to be as benevolent as possible, that he imagines them because his mind is troubled by the fear aroused in him by the presentiment of a more or less imminent ruin of Western civilization, and let us regret that he has not been able to see clearly where the real causes likely to bring about this ruin lie, even though he sometimes shows a just severity with regard to certain aspects of the modern world. On the one hand, he doesn't know exactly which adversaries he should be fighting, and on the other, his "traditionalism" leaves him blissfully unaware of the very essence of tradition, which he obviously confuses with a kind of politico-religious "conservatismof the most external order.

We say that Massis's mind is troubled by fear. Massis is troubled by fear; perhaps the best proof of this is the extraordinary, indeed quite inconceivable, attitude he attributes to his so-called "Eastern propagandists": they are said to be animated by a fierce hatred of the West, and it is to harm the latter that they strive to communicate their own doctrines to it, that is to say, to give it the gift of what they themselves hold most precious, of what constitutes, as it were, the very substance of their spirit! In the face of such a contradictory hypothesis, we can't help but stunned: the whole thesis, so painstakingly constructed, instantly collapses, and it seems that the author didn't even realize it, for we don't want to assume that he was aware such implausibility and simply relied on his readers' lack of foresight to make them accept it. You don't need to think very long or very deeply to realize that, if there are people who hate the West so much, the first thing they should do is to keep their doctrines jealously to themselves, and that all their efforts should be aimed at denying Westerners access to them. The truth, however, is quite different: the authentic representatives of traditional doctrines feel no hatred for anyone, and their reserve has only one cause: they consider it perfectly useless to expose certain truths to those who are incapable of understanding them; but they have never refused share them with those, whatever their origin, who possess the requisite "qualifications"; is it their fault if, among the latter, there are very few Westerners? And, the other hand, if the Eastern IIIasse ends up being truly hostile to Westerners, after having looked on them with indifference for a long time, who is to blame? Is it this elite who, all in intellectual contemplation, resolutely keeps their distance from outside agitation, or is it not rather the Westerners themselves, who have done necessary to make their presence odious and intolerable? It's enough for the question to posed as it should be, for anyone to be able to answer it immediately; and, admitting that the Orientals, who have hitherto shown incredible patience, finally want to be the masters at home, who could sincerely think of blaming them? It's true that, when certain passions get involved, the same things can, depending on the circumstances, be appreciated in very different ways, and even in the opposite direction: thus, when resistance to a foreign encroachment is shown by a Western people, it's called "patriotism" and is worthy of all praise; when it's shown by an Eastern people, it's called "fanaticism" or "xenophobia" and deserves only hatred or contempt. Besides, isn't it in the name of "Law", "Freedom", Justice" and "Civilization" that Europeans claim to impose their domination everywhere, forbid any human being to live and think differently than they themselves ? We agree that "moralism" is a truly admirable thing, unless we prefer to conclude quite simply, as we ourselves do, that, apart from a few exceptions that are all the more honourable for being rarer, there are now only two kinds of people in the West, both of them rather uninteresting: the naïve who for these grand words and believe in their "civilizing mission", unaware as they are of the materialistic barbarism into which they are plunged, and the clever who exploit this state of mind satisfy their instincts of violence and greed. In any case, what is certain is that the Orientals are not threatening anyone, nor are they thinking of invading the West in any way; for the time being, they have enough to do to defend themselves against European oppression, which threatens to reach into their very souls; and it is at least curious to see the aggressors pose as victims.

This clarification was necessary, because there are certain things that need to be said; but we would be remiss if we insisted on it any further, as the thesis of the "defenders of the West" is really too fragile and inconsistent. Incidentally, if we have departed for a moment from our usual reserve with regard to individuals to quote Henri Massis, it is mainly because he represents a certain part of the contemporary mentality, which we must also take into account in this study of the state of the modern world. How can this lower-order "traditionalism", narrow-minded and incomprehensible, per- haps even rather artificial, truly and effectively oppose a mind with which it shares so many prejudices? It's the same inability to understand the existence of different civilizations, the same superstition of Greco-Latin "classi-cism". This inadequate reaction is only of interest to us in that it marks a certain dissatisfaction with the present state of affairs among some of our contemporaries; and are other manifestations of this same dissatisfaction that would be ca-pable of going further well directed; but, for the moment, it's all very chaotic, and it's still very difficult to say what will emerge. However, a few predictions in this respect may not be entirely useless; and, as they are closely linked to the des-tiny of the present world, they may at the same time serve as conclusions for the present study, insofar as it is permissible to draw conclusions from them without giving "lay" igno-rance the opportunity for too easy attacks, by imprudently developing considerations which it would be impossible to justify by ordinary means. We are not among those who be-lieve that everything can be said indiscriminately, at least when we leave pure doctrine to come to applications; there are then certain reservations that be made, and questions of expediency that must inevitably arise; but these legitimate, and even indispensable, reservations have nothing in com-mon with certain puerile fears that are only the effect of an ignorance comparable to that of a man who, according to the proverbial Hindu expression, "mistakes a rope for a snake". Whether we like it or not, what needs to be said will be said as circumstances demand; neither the self-interested efforts of some, nor the unconscious hostility of others, will be able to prevent it from being so, any more than, on the other hand, the impatience of those who, driven by the feverish haste of the modern world, would like to know everything at once, will be able to make certain things known to the outside world sooner than is appropriate; But they can at least con-sole themselves with the thought that the accelerated course of events will doubtless give them a fairly prompt

131

satisfaction; may they not then have to regret having insufficiently prepared themselves to receive knowledge which they too often seek with more enthusiasm than true discernment!

---

1 - *Satan*, in Hebrew, is the "adversary", the one who overturns all things and turns them upside down, as it were; he is the spirit of negation and subversion, identified with the downward or "inferiorizing" tendency, "infernal" in the etymological sense, the very tendency that beings follow in this process of materialization according to which the whole development of modern civilization takes place.

2 - We know that Massis is not unaware of our works, but he carefully refrains from making the slightest allusion to them, because they would run counter to his thesis; at the very least, the procedure lacks candor. There is always something distressing in the spectacle of "profane" incomprehension, even though the truth of "sacred doctrine" is certainly, in itself, too high to undergo such attacks.

CHAPTER IX

SOME CONCLUSIONS

Above all, our aim here is to show how the application of traditional data makes it possible to resolve the most immediate questions currently facing us, to explain the present state of mankind on earth, and at the same time to judge according to the truth, and not according to conventional rules or sentimental preferences, everything that properly constitutes modern civilization. Moreover, we have not pretended to exhaust the subject, to treat it in all its details, nor to develop all its aspects without neglecting any; the principles from which we constantly draw our inspiration oblige us to present views that are essentially synthetic, and not analytical like those of "profane" knowledge; but these views, precisely because they are synthetic, go much further in the direction of a true explanation than any kind of analysis, which in reality has little more than a simple descriptive value. In any case, we believe that we have said enough to enable those who are capable of understanding to draw at least some of the implicit consequences from what we have set out; and they must be convinced that this work will be of far greater benefit to them than a reading that would leave no room for reflection and meditation, for which, on the contrary, we have only wished to provide an appropriate starting point, a sufficient support to rise above the vain multitude of individual opinions.

It remains for us to say a few words about what we might call the practical scope of such a study. We could overlook or lose interest in this scope if we had confined ourselves to pure metaphysical doctrine, in relation to which all application is merely contingent and accidental; but here, it is precisely applications that are at stake. They are the legitimate consequences of the principles, the normal development of a doctrine which, being one and universal, must embrace all orders of reality without exception; and, at the same time, they are also, for some at least, a preparatory means of ascending to higher knowledge, as we explained in connection with "sacred science". But, in addition, it is not forbidden, when we are in the field of applications, to consider them in their own right and in their own right, provided we are never thereby led to lose sight of their connection to principles; this danger is very real, since it is from this source that the degeneration that gave rise to "profane science" results, but it does not exist for those who know that everything derives and depends entirely on pure intellectuality, and that what does not consciously derive from it can only be illusory. As we've said many times before, everything must begin with knowledge; and what appears to be the furthest thing from the practical order happens to be the most effective in this very order, for without it, here as elsewhere, it's impossible to achieve anything of real value, anything other than vain and superficial agitation. This is why, to return more specifically to the question we are dealing with at present, we can say that, if all men understood what the modern world really is, it would immediately cease to exist, for its existence, like that of ignorance and all that is limitation, is purely negative: it exists only through the negation of traditional, supra-human truth. This change would thus occur without any catastrophe, which seems almost impossible by any other route; are we wrong, then, if we assert that such knowledge is likely to have truly incalculable practical consequences? But, on the other hand, it seems unfortunately very difficult to admit that everyone would arrive at this knowledge, of which most men are certainly further away than they have ever been; it's true that this is by no means necessary, for it suffices to have an elite that is few in number, but strongly enough constituted to give direction to the masses, who would obey its suggestions without even having the slightest idea of its existence or its means of action; is the effective constitution of this elite still possible in the West?

We don't intend to go back over everything we've already had occasion to say elsewhere about the role of the intellectual elite in the various circumstances we can envisage as possible in the more or less imminent future. Let us limit ourselves to saying this: whatever the way in which the change that constitutes what can be called the passage from one world to another is accomplished, whether it involves more or less extended cycles, this change, even if it has the appearance of a sudden rupture, never implies an absolute discontinuity, for there is a causal chain that links all the cycles together. The elite we're talking about, if it manages to form itself while there's still time, could prepare for the change in such a way that it takes place under the most favorable conditions, and that the turmoil that will inevitably accompany it is somehow reduced to a minimum; but, even if this is not so, it will always have another, even more important task, that of contributing to the preservation of what must survive the present world and serve to build the future world. It's obvious that we shouldn't wait until the descent is over to prepare for the ascent, since we know that this ascent will necessarily take place, even if we can't avoid the descent ending in some cataclysm beforehand; and so, in any case, the work carried out won't be lost: it can't be lost in terms of the benefits that the elite will derive from it for themselves, but neither will it be lost in terms of its subsequent results for the whole of humanity.

Now, here's how to look at it: the elite still exists in Eastern civilizations, and, even if it is reduced more and more in the face of modern encroachment, it will still exist to the very end, because it is necessary to do so in order to preserve the deposit of tradition that cannot perish, and to ensure the transmission of everything that must be preserved. In the West, on the other hand, the elite no longer exists; we may therefore ask whether it will be reformed before the end of our era, i.e. whether the Western world, despite its deviation, will have a share in this preservation and transmission; if not, the consequence will be that its civilization will have to perish altogether, because there will no longer be any element in it that can be used for the future, because all traces of the traditional spirit will have disappeared. The question, thus posed, may be of only very secondary importance as far as the final outcome is concerned; it is nonetheless of some interest from a relative point of view, which we must take into consideration as soon as we agree to take into account the particular conditions of the period in which we live. In principle, we could be content to point out that the Western world is, after all, part of the whole from which it seems to have been detached since the beginning of modern times, and that, in the final integration of the cycle, all the parts must find each other again in some way; but this does not necessarily imply a prior restoration of the Western tradition, as this can only be preserved as a permanent possibility in its very source, outside the special form it took at a given moment. We give this only as an indication, because to understand it fully, we would have to consider the relationship between the primordial tradition and the subordinate traditions, which we cannot consider doing here. This would be the most unfavorable case for the Western world as a whole, and its current state may lead us to fear that this is the case that is actually being realized; however, we have said that there are some signs that all hope of a better solution is not yet definitively lost.

If they have been reduced to imprecise aspirations and all too often fruitless research, if they have even gone completely astray, it is because they lack real data for which nothing can make up, and because there is no organization that can provide them with the necessary doctrinal guidance. We are not, of course, talking about those who have found this guidance in Eastern traditions, and who are thus intellectually outside the Western world; these people, who can only represent an exceptional case, can in no way be an integral part of a Western elite; They are, in fact, an extension of the Eastern elites, which could become a link between the latter and the Western elite once the latter has been established.

This initiative is only possible in two ways: either the West will find the means within itself, through a direct return to its own tradition, a return which would be like a spontaneous awakening of latent possibilities; or certain Western elements will accomplish this work of restoration with the help of a certain knowledge of Eastern doctrines, knowledge which however cannot be absolutely immediate for them, since they must remain Western, but which can be obtained through a kind of second degree influence, exerted through intermediaries such as those we alluded to earlier. The first of these two hypotheses is highly implausible, since it implies the existence, in the West, of at least one point where the traditional spirit would have been preserved in its entirety, and we have said that, despite certain assertions, this existence seems to us extremely doubtful; it is therefore the second hypothesis that we should examine more closely.

In this case, it would be advantageous, though not absolutely necessary, for the elite in training to be able to find a base in a Western organization that already exists; and it would seem that there is now only one organization in the West that has a traditional character, and that retains a doctrine capable of providing the work in question with an appropriate foundation: the Catholic Church. It would suffice to restore to its doctrine, without changing the religious form in which it is presented to the outside world, the profound meaning it really has in itself, but of which its current representatives no longer seem to be aware, nor of its essential unity with the other traditional forms; the two things, moreover, are inseparable from each other. This would be the realization of Catholicism in the true sense of the word, which etymologically expresses the idea of "universality", something that is too often forgotten by those who would like to see it as the exclusive denomination of a special, purely Western form, with no effective link to other traditions; and it can be said that, in the present state of affairs, Catholicism has only a virtual existence, since we do not really find in it an awareness of universality; but it is no less true that the existence of an organization which bears such a name is an indication of a possible basis for a restoration of the traditional spirit in its full sense, and all the more so since, in the Middle Ages, it already served as a support for this spirit in the Western world. So, in short, it's nothing more than a reconstitution of what existed before the modern deviation, with the necessary adaptations to the conditions of another era; and if some people are astonished or protest against such an idea, it's because they are themselves, unwittingly and perhaps unwillingly, imbued with the modern spirit to the point of having completely lost the sense of a tradition of which they retain only the bark. It would be important to know whether the formalism of the "letter", which is still one of the varieties of "materialism" as we understood it earlier, has definitively suffocated spirituality, or whether the latter is only temporarily obscured and can still be reawakened in the very heart of the existing organization.

It may be, moreover, that these events themselves will sooner or later impose on the leaders of the Catholic Church, as an inescapable necessity, something whose importance they would not directly understand from the point of view of pure intellectuality; it would certainly be regrettable if circumstances as contingent as those of the political sphere, considered outside any higher principle, were needed to give them food for thought; but it must be admitted that the opportunity for the development of latent possibilities must be provided to everyone by the means that are most immediately within the reach of their present understanding. That's why we'll say this: in the face of worsening disorder, which is becoming more and more generalized, we must call upon the union of all spiritual forces still active in the outside world, in the West as well as in the East; and, on the Western side, we see no other than the Catholic Church. If the Catholic Church could thereby make contact with the representatives of Eastern traditions, we could only congratulate ourselves on this first result, which could be precisely the starting point for what we have in mind, since it would no doubt soon be realized that a merely external and "diplomatic" understanding would be illusory and could not have the desired consequences, The necessary and sufficient condition for this would be for the representatives of the West to become truly aware of these principles, as those of the East always are. True agreement, let us repeat once again, can only be achieved from above and from within, i.e. in the realm that can be called either intellectual or spiritual, because, for us, these two words basically mean exactly the same thing; then, and starting from there, the agreement would also necessarily be established in all other fields, just as, once a principle has been laid down, all that remains to be done is to deduce, or rather "explain", all the consequences implied by it. There can be only one obstacle to this: Western proselytism, which cannot bring itself to admit that we must sometimes have "allies" who are not "subjects"; or, to put it more accurately, it is the lack of understanding of which this proselytism is only one of the effects; will this obstacle be overcome? If it were not, the elite would have to rely solely on the efforts of those qualified by their intellectual capacity, outside any defined milieu, and also, of course, on the support of the East; its work would be made more difficult and its action could only be carried out over a longer period of time, since it would have to create all the instruments itself, instead of finding them ready-made as in the other case; but we in no way think that these difficulties, however great they may be, are such as to prevent what must be accomplished one way or another.

We therefore feel it opportune to state the following: there are already clear signs of a movement in the Western world, which is as yet imprecise, but which can and should lead to the reconstitution of an intellectual elite, unless a cataclysm occurs too quickly to allow it to develop to its full potential. Needless to say, it would be in the Church's interest to anticipate such a movement, rather than let it take place without her, and be forced to follow it at a late stage to maintain an influence that would threaten to slip away; You don't have to take a very high and inaccessible viewpoint to understand that, all in all, it is she who would have the greatest advantages to gain from an attitude which, moreover, far from requiring the slightest compromise on her part in the doctrinal order, would, on the contrary, have the result of ridding her of any infiltration of the modern spirit, and by which, moreover, nothing would be modified externally. It would be somewhat paradoxical to see integral Catholicism realized without the help of the Catholic Church, which would then perhaps find itself in the singular obligation of accepting to be defended, against assaults more terrible than those it has ever suffered, by men whom its leaders, or at least those they allow to speak in their name, would have first sought to discredit by casting on them the most ill-founded suspicion; and, for our part, we would regret it if it were so; but, if we do not want things to come to this point, it is high time for those whose position confers the most serious responsibilities, to act with full knowledge of the facts, and no longer allow attempts which may have consequences of the utmost importance to be stopped by the incomprehension or malice of a few more or less subordinate individualities, as has already happened, and which shows once again the extent to which disorder reigns everywhere today. We anticipate that no one will be grateful to us for these warnings, which we give in a completely independent and disinterested way; it doesn't matter to us, and we will continue, when necessary, and in the form we deem best suited to the circumstances, to say what needs to be said. What we are saying at present is merely a summary of the conclusions we have reached through certain very recent "experiments", undertaken, it goes without saying, on purely intellectual ground; we have no need, for the moment at least, to go into details which, moreover, would be of little interest in themselves; but we can affirm that there is not a single word in the foregoing that we have written without having given it careful thought. Let it be known that it would be perfectly pointless to try to oppose this with philosophical arguments that we wish to ignore; We are talking seriously about serious things, we have no time to waste on verbal discussions that are of no interest to us, and we intend to remain entirely alien to all polemics, all school or party quarrels, just as we absolutely refuse to let any Western label be applied to us, for there is none that suits us; whether it pleases or displeases some, that's the way it is, and nothing can make us change our attitude in this respect. We must now also sound a warning to those who, by their aptitude for higher understanding, if not by the degree of knowledge they have actually attained, seem destined to become elements of the possible elite. There can be no doubt that the modern mind, which is truly "diabolical" in every sense of the word, is doing its utmost to prevent these elements, now isolated and dispersed, from acquiring the cohesion they need to exert a real influence on the general mentality. It is therefore up to those who have already, more or less fully, become aware of the goal towards which their efforts should be directed, not to let themselves be diverted by the difficulties, whatever they may be, that lie ahead. For those who have not yet reached the point at which infallible guidance makes it impossible to deviate from the true path, the most serious deviations are always to be feared. The greatest prudence is therefore necessary, and we would even go so far as to say that it must be pushed to the point of mistrust, for the "adversary", who up to this point has not been definitively defeated, can take the most diverse and sometimes the most unexpected forms. Those who believe they have escaped from modern "materialism" are sometimes taken back by things which, while appearing to oppose it, are in fact of the same order; and, given the turn of mind of Westerners, it is appropriate in this respect to warn them in particular against the attraction that more or less extraordinary "phenomena" can exert on them; This is the source of most of the "neo-spiritualist" errors, and it is to be expected that this danger will become even more acute, as the dark forces that maintain the current disorder find in it one of their most powerful means of action. It is even likely that we are no longer very far from the time to which this gospel prediction, which we have already recalled elsewhere, refers: "False Christs and false prophets will arise, who will perform great wonders and astonishing things, to the point of seducing, if it were possible, the very elect." The "elect" are, as the word indicates, those who belong to the "elite" understood in the fullness of its true meaning, and indeed, let us say on this occasion, this is why we hold to the term "elite" despite the abuse that is made of it in the "profane" world ; these, by virtue of the inner "realization" they have achieved, can no longer be seduced, but the same cannot be said of those who, having only the potential for knowledge within them, are properly only "called"; We are entering a time when it will be particularly difficult to "distinguish the chaff from the wheat", to really carry out what theologians call "discernment of spirits", because of the disordered manifestations that will only intensify and multiply, and also because of the lack of true knowledge among those whose normal function should be to guide others, and who today are all too often no more than "blind guides". We shall then see whether, in such circumstances, dialectical subtleties are of any use, and whether a "philosophy", even the best possible, will suffice to stop the unleashing of the "infernal powers"; This, too, is an illusion against which some have to defend themselves, for there are too many people who, unaware of what pure intellectuality is, imagine that merely philosophical knowledge - which, even in the most favourable case, is barely a shadow of true knowledge, is capable of remedying everything and straightening out the contemporary mentality, just as there are those who believe they find in modern science itself a means of ascending to higher truths, when this science is founded precisely on the negation of these truths. All these illusions are just as many causes of misguidance; many efforts are thus spent in pure loss, and it is in this way that many who would sincerely like to react against the modern spirit are reduced to impotence, because, having failed to find the essential principles without which all action is absolutely vain, they have let themselves be drawn into dead ends from which it is no longer possible for them to escape.

Those who manage to overcome all these obstacles, and to triumph over the hostility of an environment opposed to all spirituality, will doubtless be few in number; but, once again, it's not the number that matters, for we are dealing here with a domain whose laws are quite different from those of matter. There is therefore no reason to despair; and, even if there were no hope of achieving any appreciable result before the modern world sinks into some catastrophe, this would still not be a valid reason for not undertaking a work whose real scope extends far beyond the present era. Those tempted to give in to discouragement must remember that nothing accomplished in this order can ever be lost, that disorder, error and obscurity can prevail only in appearance and only momentarily, that all partial and transitory imbalances must necessarily contribute to the great total equilibrium, and that nothing can ultimately prevail against the power of truth; their motto must be that once adopted by certain initiatic organizations in the West: *Vincit omnia Veritas*.

RENÉ GUÉNON

BIOGRAPHY

René Guénon, born November 15, 1886 in Blois, France, and died January 7, 1951 in Cairo, was a major figure in twentieth-century philosophical and spiritual thought. His work, which combines metaphysics, spirituality and criticism of modernity, had a considerable influence on various currents of thought, notably traditionalism and esotericism

Guénon grew up in a middle-class family and showed a keen interest in philosophy, religion and spiritual traditions from an early age. He pursued studies in philosophy and mathematics, but soon turned away from academic paths to explore deeper, more universal systems of thought. In 1909, he moved to Paris, where he frequented intellectual and spiritual circles, and began publishing articles in esoteric journals.

His first major work, "The Crisis of the Modern World", published in 1927, laid the foundations for his critique of modernity. In it, Guénon analyzed the disastrous consequences of the break with the spiritual and metaphysical traditions he considered essential to the equilibrium of humanity. He denounces the materialism, rationalism and individualism that characterize modern society, arguing that these trends lead to spiritual degradation and a loss of meaning.

Over the years, Guénon developed a metaphysical approach inspired by various religious traditions, including Hinduism, Christianity and Islam. His work "The Symbolism of the Cross" illustrates his ability to decipher the universal symbols present in different spiritual traditions. Guénon insists that these symbols contain profound and timeless truths that can guide humanity towards a higher understanding of reality.

In 1930, Guénon moved to Egypt, where he converted to Islam, taking the name Abd al-Wahid Yahya. This conversion marked an important stage in his life and work, as it enabled him to deepen his understanding of Eastern spiritual traditions. In Egypt, he continued to write and publish, while engaging in studies of Islam and Sufi mysticism.

Guénon's influence extends beyond his own time. His ideas have inspired many contemporary thinkers and contributed to the revival of interest in spiritual and esoteric traditions. His critical approach to modernity and his quest for timeless wisdom still resonate today, as many people seek answers to the spiritual and existential crises of the modern world.

In short, René Guénon is an emblematic figure whose work continues to provoke reflection and debate. His critique of modernity and his exploration of spiritual traditions offer a unique perspective on contemporary challenges, inviting everyone to seek a deeper understanding of themselves and the world around them.

BIBLIOGRAPHY

INTRODUCTION TO THE STUDY OF THE HINDU DOCTRINES (1921)

THEOSOPHY: HYSTORY OF A PSEUDO-RELIGION (1921)

THE SPIRITIST FALLACY (1923)

EAST AND WEST (1924)

MAN AND HIS BECOMING ACCORDING TO THE VEDANTA (1925)

THE ESOTERISM OF DANTE (1925)

THE CRISIS OF THE MODERN WORLD (1927)

THE KING OF THE WORLD (1927)

SPIRITUAL AUTHORITY AND TEMPORAL POWER (1929)

THE SYMBOLISM OF THE CROSS (1931)

THE MULTIPLE STATES OF THE BEING (1932)

THE REIGN OF QUANTITY AND SIGNS OF THE TIMES (1945)

PERSPECTIVES ON INITIATION (1946)

THE GREAT TRIAD (1946)

THE METAPHYSICAL PRINCIPLES OF THE
INFINITESIMAL CALCULUS (1946)

INITIATION AND SPIRITUAL REALIZATION (1952)

INSIGHTS INTO CHRISTIAN ESOTERISM (1954)

SYMBOLS OF SACRED SCIENCE (1962)

STUDIES IN FREEMASONRY AND THE COMPAGNONNAGE (1964)

STUDIES IN HINDUISM (1966)

TRADITIONAL FORMS AND COSMIC CYCLES (1970)

INSIGHTS INTO ISLAMIC ESOTERISM AND TAOISME (1973)

REVIEWS (1973)

MISCELLANEA (1976)

"The Reign of Quantity and the Signs of the Times" is a major work by René Guénon, published in 1945. In this book, Guénon explores the consequences of the dominance of quantification and materialism in modern society, while highlighting the signs of a profound spiritual crisis. The author begins by drawing a distinction between the traditional world, where quality and spirituality prevail, and the modern world, which is characterized by an obsession with quantity, rationalism and materialism. Guénon argues that this inversion of values has led to a degradation not only of culture, but also of human consciousness itself. He analyzes how this tendency to privilege the quantitative has infiltrated all aspects of life, including science, economics and even spirituality.

Guénon also discusses the "signs of the times", i.e. the symbolic manifestations and events that bear witness to this crisis. He refers to contemporary phenomena such as wars, social conflicts and ecological upheavals as indicators of a profound imbalance and a break with traditional principles. In his view, these signs are not simply the result of material factors, but reveal a spiritual and metaphysical dimension that deserves to be examined.

In sum, "The Reign of Quantity and the Signs of the Times" is an incisive critique of modernity, inviting reflection on the true nature of existence and the need for a return to spiritual principles to overcome the current crisis. Guénon's work remains relevant, resonating with contemporary concerns about spirituality and authenticity in a world increasingly dominated by quantity.

CONTENTS

Printed in Dunstable, United Kingdom